Windy City BAGS

12 HANDBAGS AND TOTES
~ sewn with ~
STRUCTURE AND STYLE

Sara Lawson

Martingale®
Create with Confidence

dedication

For William, Violet, and Danny. You are my entire world.

To my blog readers and pattern testers—thank you for pushing me to continue to create with joy!

Windy City Bags: 12 Handbags and Totes
Sewn with Structure and Style
© 2015 by Sara Lawson

Martingale®
19021 120th Ave. NE, Ste. 102
Bothell, WA 98011-9511 USA
ShopMartingale.com

Printed in China
20 19 18 17 16 15   8 7 6 5 4 3 2 1

Library of Congress Cataloging-in-Publication Data is available upon request.

ISBN: 978-1-60468-599-2

MISSION STATEMENT

Dedicated to providing quality products and service to inspire creativity.

CREDITS

PUBLISHER AND CHIEF VISIONARY OFFICER
Jennifer Erbe Keltner

EDITORIAL DIRECTOR
Karen Costello Soltys

MANAGING DIRECTOR
Tina Cook

ACQUISITIONS EDITOR
Karen M. Burns

TECHNICAL EDITOR
Rebecca Kemp Brent

COPY EDITOR
Tiffany Mottet

DESIGN DIRECTOR
Paula Schlosser

PHOTOGRAPHER
Brent Kane

PRODUCTION MANAGER
Regina Girard

COVER AND
INTERIOR DESIGNER
Adrienne Smitke

ILLUSTRATOR
Christine Erikson

contents

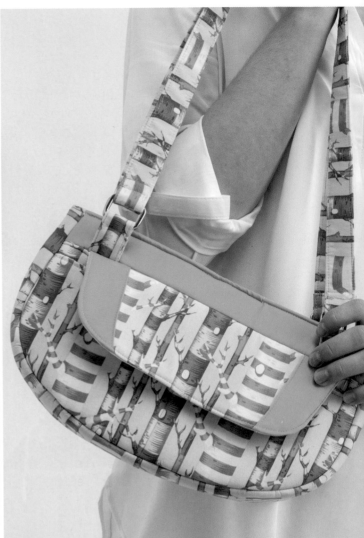

introduction

One can never have too many bags. Whether you're using the latest fabric from your local quilt shop or a long-hoarded treasure, this book will allow you to try out a variety of different modern bag shapes and sizes. Combine that with quality interfacing and perhaps a bit of purse hardware, and you'll have a conversation starter on your hands (or shoulder!).

I wrote my very first bag pattern right before Christmas of 2011. It was a free pattern for Pellon's website. At the time I had no idea where that first pattern would take me, but I'm so grateful to everyone who has ever made one of my bags. I love to see the triumph on your faces when you send me photos of you holding your finished bags. I love to hear the excitement in your voices when you make a bag that gets the attention of your entire quilt guild. That's why I do this, and I am utterly thrilled to be able to write a follow-up to my first book, *Big-City Bags*.

While all of the bags in this book are rated at an intermediate sewing level, I hope that the well-written and illustrated instructions will tempt a confident sewist of any skill level to make a bag. Rest assured, you'll find all the how-to information needed for success at the end of this book. From choosing the right type of interfacing or stabilizer to attaching a zipper, magnetic clasp, or metal purse feet, I've got the answers you'll need. Plus, check out "Choosing Fabric" on page 94 to see a gallery of color combinations and fabric options to inspire you. And all the pattern pieces are on the pullout sheets at the back of the book.

If you're trying out your first structured bag, I recommend Beguiling (page 70) or Copilot (page 64). If you're ready to step up your skills, try the Jump-Start Duffel (page 36) or the Shades Laptop Backpack (page 76).

I hope you'll enjoy making many of the bags from my book. Writing bag patterns is one of the things I love best in the world, and I hope it shows!

— *Sara*

Sara says

Look for "Sara says" boxes throughout the book for more of my favorite tips for personalizing your projects!

Hey Mercedes

With its curvy shape, Hey Mercedes fits comfortably into the crook of your arm, giving some flair to your arm candy.

FINISHED SIZE: 16" x 14" x 3½"

MATERIALS

Yardage is based on 42"-wide fabric unless otherwise noted.

1⅛ yard of lime-green solid for straps and accents

1 yard of multicolored print for exterior

1 yard of aqua print for lining

⅝ yard of 58"-wide Soft and Stable (or Thermolam Plus fusible fleece)

2⅞ yards of 20"-wide Shape-Flex fusible woven interfacing (or other medium-weight fusible interfacing)

4 metal rectangular rings (1½")

1 magnetic snap (½")

2 zippers, 12" long

CUTTING

The patterns for the main panel, front pocket, and handle extender are on pattern sheet 1.

From the multicolored print, cut:
1 rectangle, 4½" x 29", for bag bottom
2 main panels, *on fold,* for bag front and back
1 front pocket, *on fold*

From the aqua print, cut:
1 rectangle, 4½" x 29", for lining bottom
2 main panels, *on fold,* for lining front and back
1 front pocket, *on fold,* for pocket lining

From the lime-green solid, cut:
2 rectangles, 5" x 36", for handles
4 handle extenders and 4 handle extenders, reversed*
2 rectangles, 10" x 14", for lining pockets
1 strip, 1" x 12½", *on the bias*

From the Soft and Stable, cut:
1 rectangle, 4½" x 29", for bag bottom
2 main panels, *on fold,* for bag front and back**
2 squares, 1½" x 1½", for snap reinforcements

From the Shape-Flex, cut:
2 rectangles, 5" x 36", for handles
1 rectangle, 4½" x 29", for lining bottom
2 main panels, *on fold,* for lining front and back
2 front pockets, *on fold,* for pocket lining and pocket
4 handle extenders and 4 handle extenders, reversed*

To save time, fold the fabric with either right or wrong sides together and cut two handle extenders at the same time; one in each pair will be reversed.

**Because the Soft and Stable is thick, you'll be able to cut more accurately if you prepare a full pattern from a folded piece of paper and use it to cut the stabilizer in a single layer without folding. You can also use the cut fabric, unfolded, as your pattern.*

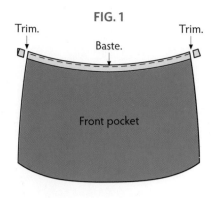

FIG. 1

Trim. Baste. Trim.

Front pocket

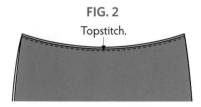

FIG. 2

Topstitch.

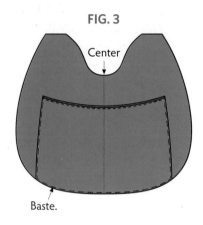

FIG. 3

Center

Baste.

* turns out

For easier turning, you can leave an opening along the inner curved edge of the handle extenders about 3" below the curved, short end. Then, after clipping and turning, press the seam allowances to the wrong side to prepare for topstitching.

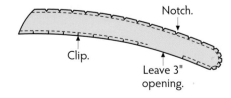

Clip. Notch. Leave 3" opening.

ATTACH THE INTERFACING

1. **Place the wrong side** of the bag bottom against the corresponding piece of Soft and Stable and pin. Baste ⅛" from the outer edge. Repeat for the bag front and back.

2. **Following the manufacturer's instructions,** fuse the Shape-Flex pieces to the wrong sides of the lining front, back, and bottom, front pocket, front-pocket lining, handles, and handle extenders.

ATTACH THE FRONT POCKET

All seam allowances are ½" unless otherwise noted.

1. **Press the 1" x 12½" bias strip** in half lengthwise with wrong sides together. Pin the folded strip to the right side of the front pocket, aligning the raw edges at the top of the pocket. Baste ⅛" from the raw edges. Trim the excess strip where it overhangs the sides of the pocket (fig. 1).

2. **Using a ¼" seam allowance,** sew the front-pocket lining to the pocket at the top (concave) edge, sandwiching the bias strip between the layers. Clip the seam allowances along the curve. Turn the pocket right side out and press, with the accent strip extending above the pocket edge. Topstitch ⅛" from the seam through all the layers (fig. 2).

3. **Finger-press the bag** front and the front pocket in half vertically to find the centerlines. Place the front pocket on the bag front, aligning the creases and the bottom raw edges. Pin in place. Baste the pocket sides and bottom edge to the bag, stitching ⅛" from the pocket raw edges (fig. 3).

MAKE THE HANDLES

1. **Press a handle** in half lengthwise, wrong sides together. Open the fold and press the long edges to the wrong side so that they meet at the crease. Refold along the original crease and press once more, concealing the long raw edges. Topstitch ⅛" from both long edges. Make two handles.

2. **Place a handle extender** on a reversed handle extender with right sides together. Sew, using a ¼" seam allowance and leaving the straight, short end open. Clip the seam allowances along the curved edges. Turn the handle extender right side out using a tube turner or long object with a rounded tip, such as a wooden spoon's handle, to smooth the curves and edges. Topstitch ⅛" from the long edges and curved, short end. Make four handle extenders. **✳ See "Turns Out," left.**

3. **Fold the curved end** of one handle extender to the outside, 3¾" below the curved end, and press. Repeat with the remaining handle extenders; be sure to make two that curve to the left and two that curve to the right (fig. 4).

4. **Transfer the handle extender placement marks** from the main-panel pattern onto both halves of the bag front and back. Place one handle extender inside the placement lines on one half of the bag front with the pressed curved end facing outward and the extender curving toward the center of the bag front. Pin in place. Lift the curved end out of the way and edgestitch along both long edges from the bottom of the bag to the crease pressed in step 3, sewing directly on top of the previous stitching and backstitching at the upper end (fig. 5).

5. **Flip the curved edge** back down as pressed. Slide one rectangular ring onto the handle extender so it lies in the fold. Topstitch the curved end of the handle extender to the bag, sewing on top of the previous stitching. Sew as close to the ring as possible (approximately ¼" away), pivot, and sew across the handle extender to the other side (fig. 6). ✳ See "Sew Close," right.

6. **Repeat steps 4 and 5** to attach the other three handle extenders.

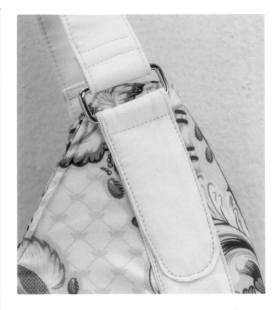

✳ *sew close*

Using a zipper foot to edgestitch the handle extender will help you sew closer to the purse hardware.

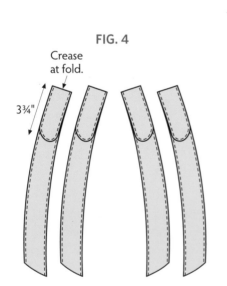

FIG. 4

Crease at fold.

3¾"

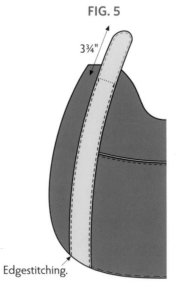

FIG. 5

3¾"

Edgestitching.

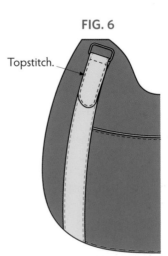

FIG. 6

Topstitch.

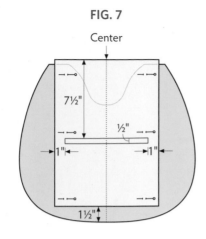

FIG. 7

Center

7½"

½"

1" 1"

1½"

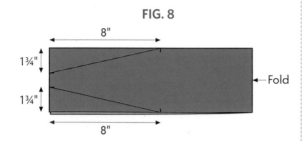

FIG. 8

8"

1¾"

1¾"

Fold

8"

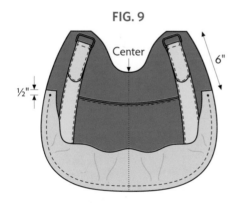

FIG. 9

Center

6"

½"

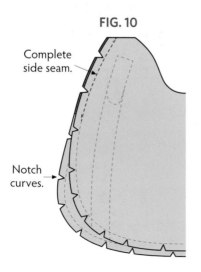

FIG. 10

Complete side seam.

Notch curves.

MAKE THE LINING POCKETS

1. **On the wrong side** of one lining pocket, measure and mark a horizontal line 7½" below the top 10"-wide edge. Draw another horizontal line ½" below the first.

2. **Draw vertical lines** 1" from each side of the pocket, connecting the horizontal lines to make a rectangular box.

3. **Finger-press the lining front** and lining pocket to find the vertical centerlines. Place the pocket on the lining front, right sides together, aligning the center creases, with the bottom raw edge of the pocket 1½" above the bottom of the lining front. Pin the pieces together (**fig. 7**).

4. **Follow the instructions** in "Zippered Pocket" on page 86 to install the zipper and complete the pocket.

5. **Repeat steps 1–4** to add the remaining zippered pocket to the back lining.

FINISH THE BAG

1. **Fold the bag bottom in half,** matching the short edges. Mark the short edges 1¾" from each side. Mark each long edge 8" below the short edges. Draw diagonal lines connecting the marks on each side. Cut along the lines through both layers to shape the ends of the bag bottom; discard the scraps. Using the bag bottom as a guide, trim the lining bottom (**fig. 8**).

2. **Finger-press the bag front** and bottom to find the vertical centerlines. Pin the bottom to the bag front with right sides together, starting at the centerlines and easing around both corners. The short ends of the bottom should fall 6" below the top of the bag front. Stitch along the pinned edge, starting and stopping ½" from the short ends of the bag bottom. Sew the bag back to the remaining long edge of the bottom in the same way (**fig. 9**).

3. **Pin the bag front and back together** at each unsewn upper side seam, matching the termination points of the existing seams. Sew the side seam from the top of the bag to the previous stitches and backstitch to reinforce the join. Clip the seam allowances along the curved edges (**fig. 10**).

4. **Following the instructions** in "Magnetic Snaps" on page 88, mark the placement for one half of the magnetic snap on the lining front, centered 1½" below the top edge, and install the snap. Repeat to install the other half of the magnetic snap on the lining back.

5. **Repeat steps 1–3** to assemble the bag lining, leaving an 8" opening in one bottom seam for turning.

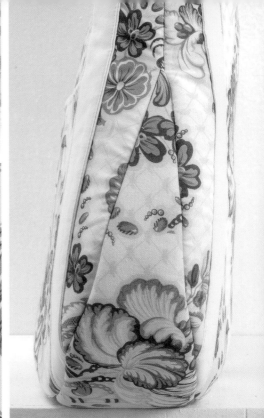

6. **Turn the bag exterior right side out** and slip the lining over the exterior so that the right sides are together. Align the top edges and side seams, tucking the handle extenders out of the way between layers. Pin and then stitch the top edge, taking special care at the side seams. Clip the seam allowances along the curves.

7. **Turn the bag right side out** through the opening in the lining and press. Topstitch ¼" from the top edge of the bag, keeping the handle extenders free. Close the opening in the lining with hand or machine stitches.

8. **Press ½" to the wrong side** on both ends of each handle. Press another 1" to the wrong side on each end.

9. **Slide one end of a handle** through a rectangular ring on the front of the bag from front to back, resting the ring in the second crease. Topstitch a small rectangular shape through all layers of the handle near the first crease to secure the ring, using a zipper foot if necessary. Repeat to secure the other end of the same handle to the second rectangular ring on the bag front. Attach the second handle to the rings on the bag back in the same way **(fig. 11)**.

FIG. 11

Topstitch.

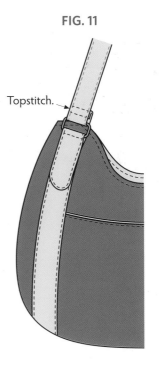

Delilah

What started as a cute idea on paper seemed way too big and clunky by the time I drafted the pattern pieces, so I returned to my original sketches and settled on this little design, featuring a detailed flap and pretty purse hardware.

FINISHED SIZE: 11" x 7" x 4"

MATERIALS

Yardage is based on 42"-wide fabric unless otherwise noted.

⅝ yard of gray print for exterior

⅜ yard of green solid for accents and lining pockets

⅜ yard of beige print for lining

⅜ yard of 58"-wide Soft and Stable (or Thermolam Plus fusible fleece)*

1⅞ yards of 20"-wide Shape-Flex fusible woven interfacing (or other medium-weight fusible interfacing)

4 metal rectangular rings (1")

2 magnetic snaps (½")

2 zippers, 9" *or* 10" long

CUTTING

The patterns for the main panel/pocket and flap are on pattern sheet 1.

From the gray print, cut:
2 rectangles, 4" x 32", for straps
1 rectangle, 5" x 23", for bag bottom
2 main panels, *on fold,* for bag front and back
1 front pocket, *on fold*
1 flap, *on fold*
4 squares, 4" x 4", for tabs

From the green solid, cut:
2 squares, 10" x 10", for zippered pockets
4 rectangles, 2¼" x 13", for bag and lining top panels
2 rectangles, 2" x 5", for flap accents

From the beige print, cut:
1 rectangle, 5" x 23", for lining bottom
2 main panels, *on fold,* for lining front and back
1 front pocket, *on fold,* for pocket lining
1 flap, *on fold,* for flap lining

From the Soft and Stable, cut:
1 rectangle, 5" x 23", for bag bottom
2 main panels, *on fold,* for front and back*
1 flap, *on fold,* for flap lining; trim ½" from the straight top edge*
2 rectangles, 2¼" x 13", for bag top panels
2 squares, 1½" x 1½", for snap reinforcement

Because the Soft and Stable is thick, you'll be able to cut more accurately if you prepare a full pattern from a folded piece of paper and use it to cut the stabilizer in a single layer without folding. You can also use the cut fabric, unfolded, as your pattern.

Continued on page 14

Continued from page 12

From the Shape-Flex, cut:
2 rectangles, 4" x 32", for straps
1 rectangle, 5" x 23", for lining bottom
2 main panels, *on fold,* for lining front and back
2 front pockets, *on fold,* for pocket lining and pocket
1 flap, *on fold*
4 squares, 4" x 4", for tabs
2 rectangles, 2¼" x 13", for lining top panels
2 rectangles, 2" x 5", for flap accents

ATTACH THE INTERFACING

1. **Place the wrong side** of the bag bottom against the corresponding piece of Soft and Stable and pin. Baste ⅛" from the outer edge. Repeat for the bag front and back, flap lining, and bag top panels. Note that the edge of the Soft and Stable lies ½" below the straight top edge of the flap lining; leave the top edge unbasted.

2. **Following the manufacturer's instructions,** fuse the Shape-Flex pieces to the wrong side of the straps, tabs, flap, flap accents, front pocket, front-pocket lining, and lining bottom, front, back, and top panels.

ASSEMBLE THE FLAP

All seam allowances are ½" unless otherwise noted.

1. **Mark a snap placement** on the lining flap, centered 1" above the curved edge. Following the manufacturer's instructions and the information in "Magnetic Snaps" on page 88, install the ball half of one magnetic snap at the mark.

2. **Press ¼" to the wrong side** along one long edge of each flap accent piece.

3. **Place one flap accent** on the flap, right sides up, aligning the long raw edge of the accent with the raw side edge of the flap. The accent piece will extend above and below the flap edges. Pin the accent to the flap. Position the second flap accent on the opposite edge of the flap. Topstitch ⅛" from the pressed edges of the accent pieces to attach the accents to the flap, continuing the stitching to baste the other edges of the accent pieces to the flap. Trim the accent pieces to match the top and bottom flap edges (fig. 1).

Sara says

For a polished touch, fussy cut the flap and bag-front pieces so the print matches along the opening.

FIG. 1

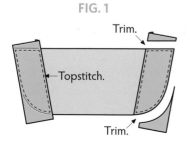

Trim.

Topstitch.

Trim.

4. **Sew the flap lining** to the flap, right sides together, with a ¼" seam allowance. Leave the straight top edge open. Notch the seam allowances along the curves to reduce bulk, being careful not to clip through the stitching.

5. **Turn the flap right side out** and press. Topstitch ⅛" from the edges of the flap, continuing across the top to hold the raw edges together.

ASSEMBLE THE BAG FRONT

1. **Sew the front pocket** and front-pocket lining together along the top edge, using a ½" seam allowance. Turn the lining to the inside, wrong sides together, and press. Topstitch ⅛" from the top edge.

2. **Place the pocket on the bag front,** right sides up, aligning the side and bottom edges, and pin. Baste ⅛" from the side and bottom edges.

3. **Finger-press the bag front** in half to find and mark the vertical centerline. Stitch along the centerline from the top of the pocket to the lower edge, dividing the pocket into two sections.

4. **Mark a snap placement** on the front pocket, centered 3" below the top edge of the bag. Install the socket half of the first magnetic snap at the mark, through all the fabric layers (fig. 2).

5. **Center the completed flap** along the top edge of the bag front, aligning the raw edges, and fasten the snap. Baste ⅛" from the upper raw edge (fig. 3).

MAKE THE STRAPS

1. **Press one strap in half lengthwise** with wrong sides together. Open the fold and press both long edges to the wrong side so that they meet at the center crease. Refold along the original crease and press once more. Topstitch ⅛" from both long edges. Make two (fig. 4).

2. **Repeat step 1** to make four tabs.

3. **Fold one tab in half,** matching the raw edges, and slide a rectangular ring into the crease. Sew across the folded tab, ¼" from the ring. Make four.

4. **Mark the upper edge** of the bag front 1¼" from each side. Lay a folded tab on the bag front, aligning the raw edges and positioning the tab to the inside of one mark. Baste ⅛" from the raw edges. Baste a second tab at the other mark on the bag front. Repeat to baste the remaining tabs to the bag back (fig. 5).

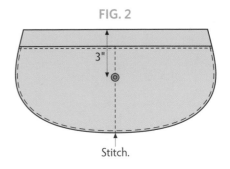

FIG. 2

3"

Stitch.

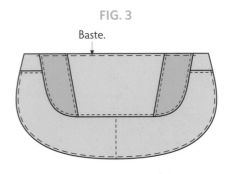

FIG. 3

Baste.

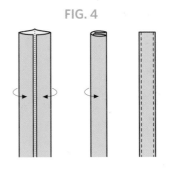

FIG. 4

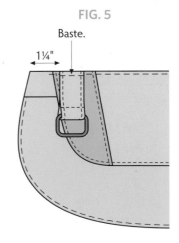

FIG. 5

Baste.

1¼"

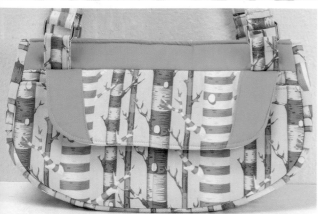

*right side up

Because the pocket pieces are square, it doesn't really matter which edge you use as the top, even if the fabric is directional. The pocket will be mostly hidden between the bag and lining.

FIG. 6

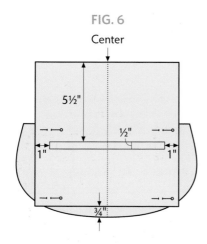

Center

5½"

½"

1"   1"

¾"

MAKE THE ZIPPERED POCKETS

1. **Draw a horizontal line** 5½" below the top edge of one zippered pocket square and a second horizontal line ½" below the first. **✳ See "Right Side Up," left.**

2. **Draw vertical lines** 1" from each side edge, connecting the horizontal lines to create a rectangular box.

3. **Finger-press the lining front** and the zippered pocket to find the vertical centerlines. Place the prepared pocket square on the lining front, right sides together, with the bottom edge of the pocket ¾" above the bottom of the lining front and the center creases aligned, and pin (fig. 6).

4. **Follow the instructions** in "Zippered Pocket" on page 86 to complete the lining pocket.

5. **Repeat steps 1–4** with the second pocket square and the lining back.

ASSEMBLE THE TOP PANEL AND LINING

1. **Center one bag top panel** on the prepared bag front with right sides together, matching the raw edges, and pin. Sew along the pinned edge (fig. 7).

2. **Press the seam allowances** toward the bag front. Open the flap and topstitch the bag front ⅛" below the seam, keeping the flap and tabs folded upward and out of the stitching. Use a ruler to extend the lines of the bag side edges diagonally through the top panel and trim along the lines (fig. 8).

3. **Repeat steps 1 and 2,** omitting the flap, to attach the remaining bag top panel to the bag back.

4. **Fold the bag bottom in half,** matching the short ends. Mark the short ends 1½" from each side. Mark each side 6" below the short ends. Draw diagonal lines connecting the marks on each side. Cut along the lines through both layers to shape the ends of the bag bottom; discard the scraps. Using the bag bottom as a guide, trim the lining bottom (fig. 9).

5. **Finger-press the bag back** to find the vertical centerline; fold the bag bottom in half widthwise to find its center. Pin the bottom to the bag back, right sides together, matching the centers. The narrow ends of the bottom should meet the upper edge of the bag back. Pin the pieces together, easing around the curves. **✱ See "Make It Ease-y," below right.**

6. **Sew along the pinned edge.** Notch the seam allowances along the curves to reduce bulk. Press the seam allowances open (fig. 10).

7. **Repeat steps 5 and 6** to attach the bag front to the other long edge of the bag bottom.

8. **Mark a snap placement** on the lining top panel, centered 1" below the top edge. Install half of the second magnetic snap at that mark, using a 1½" square of Soft and Stable as reinforcement. Repeat with the remaining lining top panel and other half of the magnetic snap.

9. **Repeat steps 1–3** and 5–7 to assemble the bag lining, leaving an 8" opening in one seam at the bottom of the lining. Fold the pockets out of the way as you sew to prevent them from becoming caught in the seams.

FIG. 7

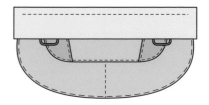

FIG. 8

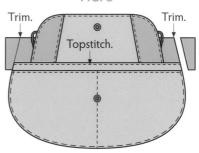

FIG. 9

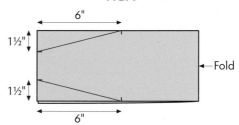

✱ make it ease-y

You may find it easier to distribute the fabric of the bottom panel if you begin pinning at the bottom center and work upward on both sides, easing the fabric as you pin.

FIG. 10

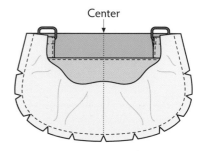

FINISH THE BAG

1. **Turn the bag right side out.** Slide the lining over the bag so that they are right sides together. Align the top edges and match the side seams. Be sure that the tabs are tucked inside, away from the top edge. Pin in place. Stitch the top edge of the bag.

2. **Turn the bag right side out** through the opening in the lining. Tuck the lining inside the bag body and press. Topstitch ⅛" from the upper edge of the bag. Close the opening in the lining by hand or machine.

3. **Press ½" to the wrong side** on both ends of each strap. Press another 1" to the wrong side on each end.

4. **Slide one end of a strap through** a rectangular ring on the front of the bag from front to back, resting the ring in the second crease. Topstitch a small rectangular shape through all layers of the strap near the first crease to secure the ring, using a zipper foot if necessary. Repeat to secure the other end of the same strap to the second rectangular ring on the bag front; be sure the strap is not twisted. Attach the second strap to the rings on the bag back in the same way (fig. 11).

FIG. 11

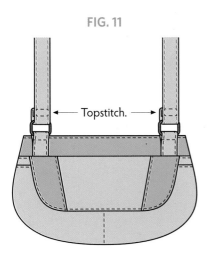

Topstitch.

Sweet Talk

Go totally retro with this '50s-style shoulder bag. It features a stiffened top panel, snap closures at the top and sides, and a zippered inner pocket. The handy front pocket is perfect for keeping your cell phone or keys within easy reach.

FINISHED SIZE: 12" x 11" x 6½"

MATERIALS

Yardage is based on 42"-wide fabric unless otherwise noted.

⅝ yard of aqua print for exterior*

½ yard of orange solid for straps, tabs, flap, and top panels

¾ yard of black print for lining

1¾ yards of 20"-wide Shape-Flex fusible woven interfacing (or other medium-weight fusible interfacing)

⅓ yard of 58"-wide Soft and Stable (or needled fusible fleece, such as Thermolam Plus)**

⅝ yard of 20"-wide Décor Bond fusible interfacing

¼ yard of Thermolam Plus fusible fleece**

4 magnetic snaps (½")

4 metal O-rings (1½")

1 zipper, 9" long

Optional: 4 metal purse feet

The yardage is sufficient for cutting a directional print like the one in the sample shown on page 20.

** See "Perfectly Stable" on page 21.

CUTTING

The patterns for the side panel, top panel, and flap are on pattern sheet 1.

From the aqua print, cut:
2 rectangles, 10¼" x 13", for bag front and back
2 side panels, *on fold*
1 rectangle, 5½" x 13", for bag bottom
1 rectangle, 6" x 8", for pocket

From the orange solid, cut:
2 rectangles, 5" x 27", for straps
4 top panels, *on fold*
1 flap, *on fold*
8 rectangles, 1¾" x 4", for tabs

From the black print, cut:
2 rectangles, 10¼" x 13", for lining front and back
2 side panels, *on fold,* for lining sides
1 rectangle, 5½" x 13", for lining bottom
1 rectangle, 6" x 8", for pocket lining
1 flap, *on fold,* for flap lining
1 rectangle, 10" x 16", for zippered pocket

From the Shape-Flex, cut:
2 rectangles, 5" x 27", for straps
2 rectangles, 10¼" x 13", for lining front and back
2 side panels, *on fold,* for lining sides
1 rectangle, 5½" x 13", for lining bottom
1 rectangle, 6" x 8", for pocket lining
4 top panels, *on fold*
1 flap, *on fold*
8 rectangles, 1¾" x 4", for tabs

Continued on page 21

Continued from page 19

From the Soft and Stable, cut:

2 rectangles, 10¼" x 13", for bag front and back

1 rectangle, 5½" x 13", for bag bottom

1 rectangle, 6" x 8", for pocket

1 flap, *on fold,* for flap lining

From the Décor Bond, cut:

1 top panel, *on fold;* trim ¼" from all edges. Using this as a pattern, cut 7 more pieces (8 total).

From the Thermolam Plus, cut:

2 side panels, *on fold*

ATTACH THE INTERFACING

1. **Place the wrong side** of the bag front against the corresponding piece of Soft and Stable and pin. Baste ⅛" from the edges. Repeat to baste Soft and Stable to the bag back and bottom, pocket, and flap lining.

2. **Following the manufacturer's instructions,** fuse Shape-Flex to the wrong sides of the straps; lining front, back, sides, and bottom; pocket lining; top panels; flap; and tabs.

3. **Center a piece of Décor Bond** on the wrong side of one top panel, on top of the previously applied Shape-Flex, and fuse. Fuse a second piece of Décor Bond directly on top of the first piece. Repeat with the remaining three top panels.

4. **Lay one Thermolam Plus side panel** on the pressing surface with the fusible side up. Cover it with a fabric side panel, right side up, and fuse. Make two.

ASSEMBLE THE TOP PANEL

All seam allowances are ½" unless otherwise noted.

1. **Sew two tab pieces,** right sides together, along both 4" edges using a ¼" seam allowance. Leave the two short ends unsewn. Turn the tab right side out and press it flat. Make four tabs.

2. **Fold one tab in half,** matching the raw edges. Slide an O-ring onto the tab, positioning it in the fold. Repeat for all four tabs.

3. **Mark the lower edge** of one top panel 2" from each side edge. Pin a prepared tab to the top panel, right sides up, with the tab just inside the mark and with raw edges aligned.

4. **Topstitch ⅛" from the tab edges,** beginning at the bottom edge of the top panel. When you reach the area with the O-ring, pivot and sew a horizontal line ¼" below the ring. Pivot again at the opposite side of the tab and continue stitching ⅛" from the tab edge, sewing to the bottom edge. ✳ See "Call it Close," right.

Sara says

Play up the retro theme by using a fun and quirky print like the mod alarm clock fabric by Melody Miller!

✳ perfectly stable

You may notice that Thermolam Plus is listed twice in the materials for this bag, once as a substitution for Soft and Stable, and then again on its own. Thermolam Plus is a bit lighter in weight than Soft and Stable, so I prefer to use it in the side panels that need to fold. If you also use it to stabilize the bag body, your Sweet Talk will be less rigid than the sample but still quite nice. However, I don't recommend using Soft and Stable in the bag's side panels.

✳ call it close

You may find that using a zipper foot to topstitch the tabs will allow you to sew closer to the purse hardware.

FIG. 1

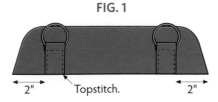

2"   Topstitch.   2"

FIG. 2

1½"

FIG. 3

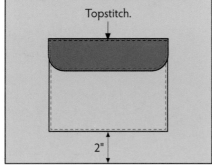

Topstitch.

2"

5. **Repeat steps 3 and 4** to attach a second tab near the other side of the same top panel. Sew the two remaining tabs to a second top panel in the same way **(fig. 1)**.

6. **Mark the snap placement** on the remaining top panels, centered 1½" above the straight bottom edge. Following the instructions in "Magnetic Snaps" on page 88, install the two halves of a magnetic snap at the marks **(fig. 2)**.

7. **Place one top panel** with tabs on a top panel with a snap, right sides together, and sew the side and top edges with a ¼" seam allowance. Notch the seam allowances along the curves, being careful not to clip through the stitching. Turn the panel right side out, and press. Topstitch ⅛" from the finished edges. Repeat with the remaining top-panel pieces.

ATTACH THE FRONT POCKET

1. **Mark a snap placement** on the front pocket, centered 1" below the top edge. Attach the socket half of the second magnetic snap at the mark. Mark a snap placement on the flap lining, centered 1" above the curved edge. Install the ball portion of the second magnetic snap at the mark.

2. **Pin the pocket to its lining,** right sides together. Sew around all sides of the pocket with a ¼" seam allowance, leaving a 4" opening along the top edge. Trim the corners diagonally to reduce bulk.

3. **Turn the pocket right side out,** using a turning tool to gently shape the corners. Press the pocket, turning the seam allowances to the wrong side along the opening. Topstitch ⅛" from the top edge, closing the opening as you stitch.

4. **Pin the flap and its lining** with right sides together. Sew around all sides with a ¼" seam allowance, leaving a 4" opening along the straight edge. Notch the seam allowances along the curved edges and clip the corners.

5. **Turn the flap right side out** and gently shape the corners and curves. Press the flap flat, turning the seam allowances to the wrong side along the opening. Topstitch ⅛" from all edges of the flap, closing the opening as you stitch.

6. **Position the prepared pocket** on the bag front, centered 2" above the bottom edge, and pin. Topstitch ⅛" from the sides and bottom edge of the pocket, leaving the top edge open.

7. **Snap the flap into place** on the front pocket and adjust it to lie straight and parallel to the bottom of the bag, then pin the upper edge of the flap in place. Topstitch ⅛" from the straight edge of the flap, sewing over the previous stitches **(fig. 3)**.

INSERT THE SNAPS IN THE BAG SIDES

Mark two snap placements on each bag side, 2" from a side edge and 1½" below the upper edge. Install the socket of one magnetic snap at the location near the left edge. Attach the corresponding ball half of the snap at the mark near the right edge of the same side piece. Attach the remaining snap to the second bag side.

ATTACH THE ZIPPERED POCKET

1. **On the wrong side** of the zippered pocket, measure and mark a horizontal line 8½" below one 10" edge. Draw a second horizontal line ½" below the first.

2. **Draw vertical lines** 1" from each side edge, creating a narrow rectangular box.

3. **Finger-press the lining back** and the pocket to find the vertical centerlines. Place the pocket on the lining back, right sides together, with the pocket's lower edge 1" above the bottom of the lining back and with centers matched, and pin (fig. 4).

4. **Following the instructions** in "Zippered Pocket" on page 86, make the zippered pocket in the lining back.

FINISH THE BAG

1. *Optional:* **Insert the purse feet** 1½" from each edge of the bag bottom, following the instructions in "Purse Feet" on page 89.

2. **Align the bottom edge** of the bag front with one long edge of the bag bottom, right sides together, and pin. Sew the long edge and press the seam allowances open. Sew the bag back to the other long edge of the bag bottom and press the seam allowances open.

3. **Find the centers** of the bottom's short edges and the side panels' bottom edges by folding and finger-pressing. Aligning the raw edges and matching the centers and top edges, pin and stitch a side panel to the assembled bag. Notch the seam allowances along the curves. Press the seam allowances open. Repeat to attach the remaining side panel to the other side of the assembled bag. ✳ See "Side Note," right.

4. **Turn the bag right side out.** Find and mark the vertical centers of the bag front and back and both top panels. Pin one top panel to the bag front with the tabs between the layers and the snap facing outward, matching the centers and aligning the long straight edges. Baste ⅛" from the straight edge. Repeat to baste the remaining top panel to the bag back (fig. 5).

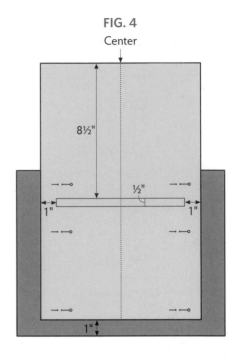

FIG. 4
Center

8½"
½"
1"   1"
1"

✳ side note

To distribute the fabric evenly, sew the sides into the bag by beginning at the bottom center and sewing up one side, then returning to the bottom center to sew up the second side. Overlap the lines of stitching at the bottom center for security.

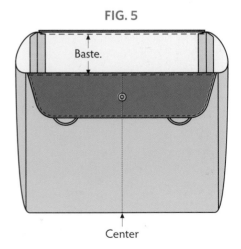

FIG. 5

Baste.

Center

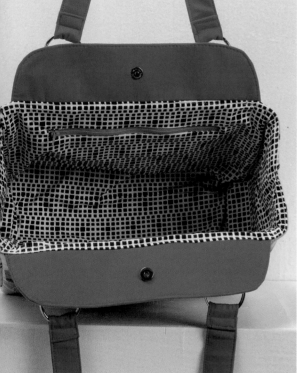

5. **Repeat steps 2 and 3** with the lining, leaving a 10" opening along one side of the lining bottom.

6. **Place the completed lining** over the exterior with right sides together. Position the lining pocket against the bag back, opposite the bag's front pocket. Tuck the top panels and tabs between the layers. Align the side seams and pin the lining to the bag. Sew the entire top edge of the bag, using a ¼" seam allowance.

7. **Turn the bag right side out** through the opening in the lining. Press the seam allowances toward the bag as you press the lining to the inside, extending the top panels away from the bag. Close the opening in the lining by hand or machine.

8. **Topstitch ⅛" below the top edge,** sewing straight across the bottom of the top panels.

9. **Press a strap in half lengthwise** with wrong sides together. Open the fold and press both long edges in to meet at the crease. Refold along the original crease and press once more. Topstitch ⅛" from each long edge. Make two. (See fig. 4 on page 15.)

10. **Press ½" to the wrong side** on each end of a strap. Press an additional 1" to the wrong side on each end. Repeat with the second strap.

11. **Slide one end of a strap** through the left O-ring on the bag front from front to back, settling the ring into the second pressed crease. Sew a small rectangular shape through all layers of the strap near the first pressed edge, securing the strap to the ring. Repeat to attach the same strap to the right O-ring on the bag front, making sure that the strap is not twisted. Attach the second strap to the O-rings on the bag back **(fig. 6)**.

FIG. 6

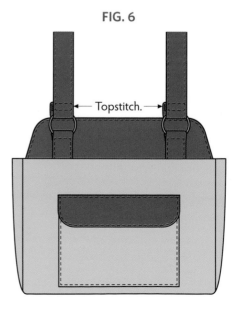

← Topstitch. →

Woodson

It's fun to use grommets in interesting ways. In this shoulder bag, a single long strap fed through all the grommets cinches the bag closed against your body but also makes for easy opening. The front pocket, with a flap and recessed zipper, is a safe place to store your essentials.

FINISHED SIZE: 12" x 8" x 4"

MATERIALS

Yardage is based on 42"-wide fabric unless otherwise noted.

¾ yard of pink print for exterior

⅝ yard of pink tone on tone for lining

⅜ yard of 58"-wide Soft and Stable (or Thermolam Plus fusible fleece)

1¼ yards of 20"-wide Shape-Flex fusible woven interfacing (or other medium-weight fusible interfacing)

1 magnetic snap (½")

4 metal grommets (1")

1 zipper, 12" long

CUTTING

The patterns for the main panel and flap are on pattern sheet 1.

From the pink print, cut:

2 strips, 2½" x 42", for strap

1 rectangle, 5" x 28¾", for bag side/bottom

2 main panels, *on fold,* for bag front and back

2 rectangles, 6" x 10½", for pocket

2 flaps, *on fold*

From the pink tone on tone, cut:

1 rectangle, 5" x 28¾", for lining side/bottom

2 main panels, *on fold,* for lining front and back

2 lining pockets, *on fold;* shorten the main-panel pattern as indicated before cutting

4 rectangles, 2" x 10½", for zipper panels

1 rectangle, 2" x 4", for zipper tab

From the Soft and Stable, cut:

1 rectangle, 5" x 28¾", for bag side/bottom

2 main panels, *on fold,* for bag front and back*

1 rectangle, 6" x 10½", for pocket

1 flap, *on fold**

From the Shape-Flex, cut:

2 strips, 2½" x 42", for strap

1 rectangle, 5" x 28¾", for lining side/bottom

2 main panels, *on fold,* for lining front and back

1 rectangle, 6" x 10½", for pocket

1 flap, *on fold*

4 rectangles, 2" x 10½", for zipper panels

*Because the Soft and Stable is thick, you'll be able to cut more accurately if you prepare a full pattern from a folded piece of paper and use it to cut the stabilizer in a single layer without folding. You can also use the cut fabric, unfolded, as your pattern.

ATTACH THE INTERFACING

1. **Pin the wrong side of the bag front** to the Soft and Stable bag-front piece. Baste ⅛" from the edges. Repeat to baste Soft and Stable to the bag back and side/bottom, one pocket, and one flap. Transfer the grommet placements from the main-panel pattern to the right side of the bag front and back.

2. **Following the manufacturer's instructions,** fuse Shape-Flex to the wrong sides of the strap pieces; lining front, back, and side/bottom; remaining pocket and flap; and zipper panels.

ASSEMBLE THE FLAP AND POCKET

All seam allowances are ½" unless otherwise noted.

1. **Mark the snap placement** on the right side of the pocket rectangle with Soft and Stable, centering it 1" below the top (long) edge of the pocket. Install the socket half of the snap, following the instructions in "Magnetic Snaps" on page 88. ✳ **See "Positive Reinforcement," right.**

2. **Pin the two pocket rectangles** right sides together. Sew along the sides and top edge, pivoting at the corners, using a ¼" seam allowance. Trim the seam allowances diagonally at the corners to reduce bulk.

3. **Turn the pocket right side out.** Use a turning tool to gently shape the corners and then press. Topstitch ⅛" from the top edge only.

4. **Center the prepared pocket** on the right side of the bag front, aligning the raw edges at the bottom. The pocket will lie 1½" from the side edges of the bag, with the snap facing outward. Topstitch ⅛" from the side edges of the pocket, continuing across the bottom edge to baste the pocket to the bag (fig. 1).

5. **Mark the snap placement** on the flap with Soft and Stable, centered 1" above the curved bottom edge of the flap. Install the ball half of the snap at the mark.

6. **Pin the two flaps** right sides together with raw edges aligned. Sew around all the edges, using a ¼" seam allowance and leaving a 6" opening at the center of the straight top edge. Trim the corners diagonally and notch the seam allowances along the curved edge, being careful not to clip through the stitching. Turn the flap right side out. Use a turning tool to gently shape the corners and curves, and then press. Topstitch ⅛" from the sides and the curved lower edge.

7. **With a removable marking tool,** draw a horizontal line 2⅜" below the top edge of the bag front. Snap the flap to the pocket and position the flap's straight edge along the line, and pin. Topstitch ⅛" and ¼" from the straight edge of the flap (fig. 2).

*positive reinforcement

Apply a 1½" square cut from a scrap of interfacing (or fusible fleece from another project) to the wrong side of the pocket and flap before installing the magnetic snaps for additional reinforcement.

FIG. 1

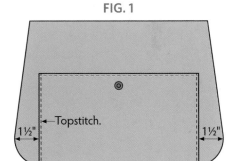

FIG. 2

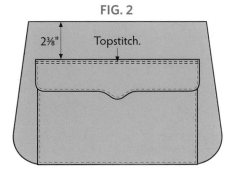

FIG. 3

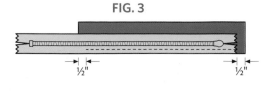

½"   ½"

FIG. 4

Topstitch.

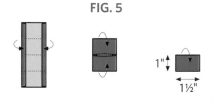

FIG. 5

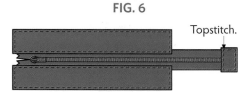

1"

1½"

FIG. 6

Topstitch.

ASSEMBLE THE LINING POCKET

1. **Pin the lining pocket pieces** right sides together. Sew along the top edge only, using a ¼" seam allowance.

2. **Press the seam allowances open,** and then fold the pieces along the seam so that they are wrong sides together; press. Topstitch ⅛" from the finished edge of the lining pocket.

3. **Place the lining pocket** on the lining back, right sides up, aligning the side and bottom raw edges, and pin. Baste ¼" from the raw edges.

4. **Finger-press the lining back** to find the vertical centerline. Topstitch on the crease from the top of the pocket to the lower edge, dividing the lining pocket into two sections.

ASSEMBLE THE ZIPPER UNIT

1. **Pin the zipper to one zipper panel,** right sides together, with the top of the zipper tape ½" from one short end of the zipper panel and the long edges aligned. The bottom of the zipper will extend beyond the other end of the zipper panel. Using a zipper foot on your sewing machine, sew the zipper to the panel, beginning and ending ½" from the short ends of the zipper panel, stitching ¼" from the zipper teeth **(fig. 3)**.

2. **Place a second zipper panel** on the first, right sides together, aligning the raw edges. The zipper will lie between the two zipper panels. Sew directly on top of the stitches from step 1.

3. **Press ¼" to the wrong side** along each raw edge of both zipper panels. Open up the zipper panels so that they are wrong sides together and the zipper is now exposed. Align the pressed edges, press, and then pin the pressed edges together, enclosing the raw edges. Topstitch ⅛" from the three pressed edges and the zipper teeth **(fig. 4)**.

4. **Repeat steps 1–3** to attach the other two zipper panels to the other side of the zipper, aligning the panels across the zipper.

5. **Press ¼" to the wrong side** on each long edge of the zipper tab. Fold the zipper tab in half, wrong sides together, matching the raw edges. Open the fold and press the raw edges in to meet at the crease. Refold along the original crease and press once more to create a 1" x 1½" folded rectangle **(fig. 5)**.

6. **Slide the bottom end of the zipper** into the zipper tab. The ends of the zipper tape should rest against the center crease, but the zipper stop must be away from the stitching line; trim the end of the zipper tape if necessary to hide the metal zipper stop inside the zipper tab. Pin the tab to the zipper.

7. **Topstitch ⅛" from all four edges** of the zipper tab. Sew slowly and carefully across the zipper teeth (turn the flywheel by hand, if necessary) to avoid breaking the needle **(fig. 6)**.

8. **Draw horizontal guidelines** 1½" below the top edge of the lining front and back. Finger-press the lining pieces and zipper panels to find their vertical centerlines.

9. **Place the assembled zipper unit** on the lining front, right sides together and centers matched, with one long edge of the zipper panel pointed toward the bottom of the bag and lying along the guideline. Sew ⅛" from the edge of the zipper panel, over the previous stitches, to attach the zipper panel to the lining front **(fig. 7)**.

10. **Sew the free edge** of the zipper panel to the lining back in the same way.

ASSEMBLE THE BAG AND LINING

1. **Fold the bag side/bottom in half,** matching the short ends. Mark the short ends 1" from each side. Mark each side 9" below the short ends. Draw diagonal lines connecting the marks on each side. Cut along the lines to shape the ends of the bag side/bottom. Baste the fabric to the stabilizer ⅛" from each of the newly cut edges. Using the bag side/bottom as a guide, trim the lining side/bottom to match **(fig. 8)**.

2. **Find and mark the bottom center** of the bag back, front, and side/bottom pieces.

3. **Pin the bag back to the side/bottom,** right sides together, matching the centers and top edges and aligning the raw edges. Ease the fabric as necessary to fit. Sew the pieces together, clip the seam allowances along the curves, and press the seam allowances open **(fig. 9)**.

4. **Sew the bag front** to the remaining long edge of the side/bottom in the same way. Repeat steps 2 and 3 with the lining pieces to assemble the lining, leaving a 6" opening at the center of one lining seam.

5. **Turn the bag right side out.** Slide the lining over the bag, right sides together. Align the top edges and seams, and then pin. Be sure the zipper panel and zipper tail will not be caught in the seam. Stitch around the top edge of the bag.

6. **Turn the bag right side out** through the opening in the lining. Press the lining to the inside along the top edge. Topstitch ¼" from the upper edge of the bag. Close the opening in the lining by hand or machine.

FIG. 7

Center

FIG. 8

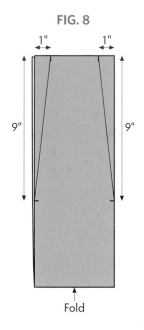

1"   1"

9"   9"

Fold

FIG. 9

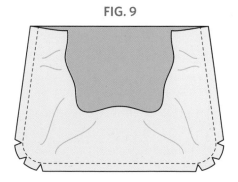

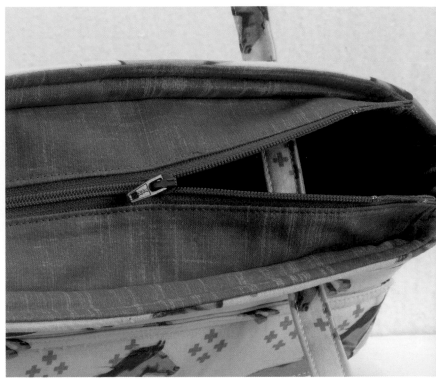

* grommet tips

The instructions on a package of grommets may state to trace and cut a circle using a provided template before installing the grommet; this is not the same as the circular placement symbol on the pattern. Please consult your grommet packaging before cutting to learn the specifics.

Sometimes the bag interfacing is too thick to allow the grommet to click into place properly. If your grommet won't fasten securely, trim the *interfacing only* from the edges of the grommet hole, making a flat area for the grommet to grab. You'll probably need to remove only the thickest interfacing, like the Soft and Stable; leave the Shape-Flex in place to reinforce the grommet opening. Don't trim the fabric!

INSERT THE GROMMETS AND STRAP

1. **Center one grommet** over the first placement marking on the bag front. Be sure the lining is smoothly positioned behind the mark. Following the manufacturer's instructions, install the grommet at the mark, through both the bag and lining. **✱ See "Grommet Tips," left.**

2. **Repeat step 1** to install grommets at the other three placement marks on the bag front and back.

3. **Join the two strap pieces,** right sides together, along one short end, using a ¼" seam allowance. Press the seam allowances open. Press the strap in half lengthwise with the wrong sides together. Open the fold and press both long edges inward to meet at the crease; press again. Refold the strip along the first crease, enclosing the long raw edges, and press once more.

4. **Topstitch ⅛" from both long edges,** leaving 2" unsewn at each end of the strip.

5. **Thread the strap through the grommets** along a circular path, passing the strap through the bag under the zipper panel.

6. **Temporarily open both ends of the strap.** Pin the ends right sides together, making sure the strap is not twisted, and sew using a ¼" seam allowance. Press the seam allowances open. Refold the strap at the join and complete the topstitching from step 4.

Clarity

This medium-sized bag is quick to sew, and the purchased faux-leather handles make it something special. Choose long handles to carry the bag on your shoulder or shorter ones, as shown here, to carry on your arm. Zippered lining pockets provide safe storage inside and solid-color accents make the main fabric pop!

FINISHED SIZE: 11½" x 8" x 6½"

MATERIALS

Yardage is based on 42"-wide fabric unless otherwise noted.

⅝ yard of blue print #1 for exterior

⅜ yard of blue solid for accents

1 yard of blue print #2 for lining*

⅜ yard of 58"-wide Soft and Stable (or Thermolam Plus fusible fleece)

1¼ yards of 20"-wide Shape-Flex fusible woven interfacing (or other medium-weight fusible interfacing)

1 pair of 16" handles with pre-punched tabs (or other length, if preferred)

1 zipper, 14" long

2 zippers, 9" long

Optional: 4 metal purse feet

*Extra fabric is included for cutting the lining pockets on the lengthwise grain.

CUTTING

The patterns for the main panel, bottom, and bottom accent are on pattern sheet 2.

From blue print #1, cut:
2 main panels, *on fold,* for bag front and back

From blue print #2, cut:
2 main panels, *on fold,* for lining front and back
1 bottom, *on fold,* for lining bottom
2 rectangles, 10" x 16", for pockets

From the blue solid, cut:
1 bottom, *on fold,* for bag bottom
2 bottom accents, *on fold*
2 rectangles, 1¾" x 15", for top accents
2 rectangles, 1½" x 3", for zipper tabs

From the Soft and Stable, cut:
2 main panels, *on fold,* for bag front and back*
1 bottom, *on fold,* for bag bottom*

From the Shape-Flex, cut:
2 main panels, *on fold,* for lining front and back
1 bottom, *on fold,* for lining bottom
2 bottom accents, *on fold*
2 rectangles, 1¾" x 15", for top accents

*Because the Soft and Stable is thick, you'll be able to cut more accurately if you prepare a full pattern from a folded piece of paper and use it to cut the stabilizer in a single layer without folding. You can also use the cut fabric, unfolded, as your pattern.

ATTACH THE INTERFACING

1. **Pin the wrong side of the bag front** to the corresponding piece of Soft and Stable. Baste ⅛" from the edges. Repeat to baste Soft and Stable to the bag back and bottom.

2. **Following the manufacturer's instructions,** fuse the Shape-Flex pieces to the wrong side of the lining bottom, front, and back, and the top and bottom accents.

ATTACH THE ACCENTS

All seam allowances are ½" unless otherwise noted.

1. **Press ¼" to the wrong side** along the bottom edge of each top-accent rectangle. Center one top accent on the bag front, aligning the top raw edges, and pin. Topstitch ⅛" from the pressed bottom edge of the accent, continuing to stitch ⅛" from the bag edges across the sides and top edge of the accent piece. Trim the ends of the accent piece to match the bag front **(fig. 1)**.

2. **Stitch ¼" from the concave top edge** of the bottom accent. Turn the raw edge to the wrong side along the stitches and press **(fig. 2)**.

3. **Place the bottom accent on the bag front,** aligning the bottom raw edges, and pin. Topstitch ⅛" from all the edges of the bottom accent **(fig. 3)**.

4. **Repeat steps 1–3** to attach the remaining top and bottom accents to the bag back.

ATTACH THE HANDLES

1. **Audition the handle placement** on your bag front. In the sample bag, the lower tip of the handle tab is 2½" below the upper edge and 4" from the side edge of the bag; adjust the placement as necessary for the size and shape of your handle tabs. Use a tool that creates removable marks to trace around the outer edge of the handle tab to mark its placement. Repeat to mark the other three tab placements, matching the measurements **(fig. 4)**.

2. **Thread two hand-sewing needles** with tapestry thread or two or three strands of all-purpose thread.

3. **Position a handle tab on the bag.** Bring the first needle through the bag and the top left hole of the handle tab from the wrong side. Take the second needle through the same hole and the bag from the right side. Weave the needles in and out of the holes, alternating the needles, until you have sewn completely around the tab to the upper right hole.

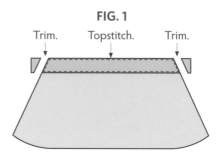

FIG. 1

Trim.   Topstitch.   Trim.

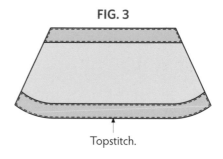

FIG. 2

¼"

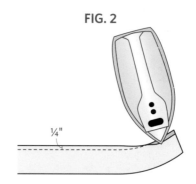

FIG. 3

Topstitch.

FIG. 4

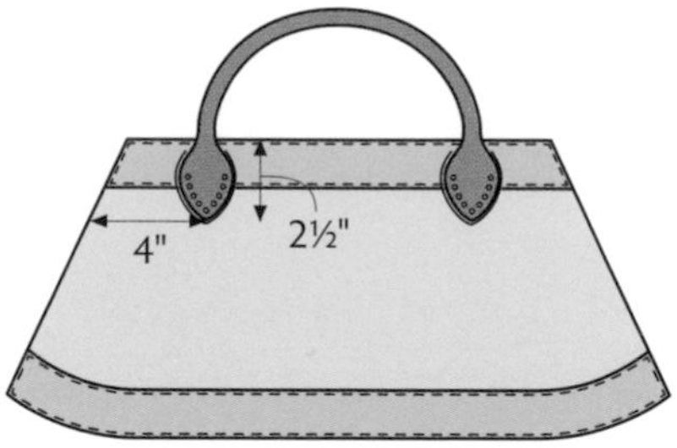

4"   2½"

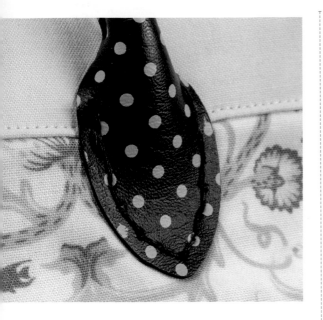

FIG. 5

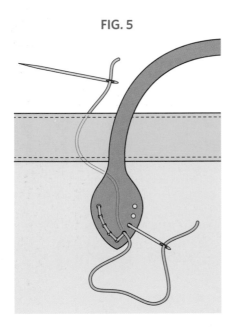

FIG. 6

Center

8½"

½"

1"   1"

½"

4. **Take all the thread tails** to the wrong side of the bag and fasten them securely **(fig. 5)**.

ASSEMBLE THE LINING POCKETS

1. **On the wrong side of one pocket,** measure and mark a horizontal line 8½" below the top 10" edge. Draw another horizontal line ½" below the first.

2. **Draw vertical lines 1" from each side edge,** connecting the horizontal lines to make a narrow rectangular box.

3. **Finger-press the lining front and pocket** to find the vertical centerlines. Place the pocket on the lining front, right sides together, with the bottom raw edge of the pocket ½" above the bottom edge of the lining front and the centerlines matched. Pin in place **(fig. 6)**.

4. **Following the "Zippered Pocket" instructions** on page 86, make the zippered pocket in the lining front using the 9"-long zipper. Repeat to make a zippered pocket in the lining back.

ATTACH THE TOP ZIPPER

1. **Measure the 14"-long zipper** and mark exactly 12¼" from the top edge of the zipper tape (not the teeth). Take a few stitches across the zipper teeth just inside the mark so that the slider can't accidentally slide off the teeth, and then trim the zipper at the mark.

2. **Press one zipper tab in half,** wrong sides together, matching the short edges. Open the fold and press both short edges inward to meet at the center crease. Refold along the original crease and press once more. Make two.

3. **Slide one end of the zipper into a zipper tab** so that the end of the zipper meets the center crease and pin. Topstitch ⅛" from the folds where they meet the zipper, securing the folded edges of the tab to the zipper. Stitch slowly and carefully over the zipper teeth (turn the flywheel by hand, if necessary) to avoid breaking the needle. Repeat to finish the other end of the zipper with the remaining zipper tab.

4. **Trim the excess fabric from the zipper tabs** on both sides of the zipper so that the tabs are the same width as the zipper.

5. **Center the assembled zipper unit** on the bag front, right sides together, with the edge of the zipper and the top edge of the bag aligned; the bag will extend ½" beyond the zipper tabs on each end. Using a zipper foot, sew the assembled zipper unit to the top edge of the bag front, using a ¼" seam allowance (fig. 7).

6. **Pin the lining front to the bag front,** right sides together, with the zipper between the layers and the top edges aligned. Sew directly on top of the stitching from the previous step, keeping the handles out of the seam and continuing the stitches all the way to the side edges.

7. **Turn the lining to the inside** so that the fabrics are wrong sides together and press. Topstitch ⅛" from the pressed edge along the length of the assembled zipper unit only.

8. **Repeat steps 5–7** to attach the other side of the zipper to the bag and lining backs. Unzip the zipper.

9. **Arrange the fabrics** so that the bag front and back are right sides together and the lining front and back are right sides together and pin. Be sure the accent edges match at the side seams. Sew the sides of the bag exterior and lining, keeping the zipper tabs out of the seams. Press the seam allowances open.

ASSEMBLE THE BAG

1. *Optional:* **Install the purse feet** as instructed in "Purse Feet" on page 89, 1½" from the edges of the bag bottom.

2. **Fold the bag bottom** to find the centers of all four sides and mark. Arrange the assembled bag so that it forms a large tube; check to be sure the zipper is still open. Pin the bottom edge of the bag exterior to the bag bottom, matching the center front and back and positioning the side seams at the side centers on the bottom piece. Ease the curved edges to fit as you pin (fig. 8).

3. **Sew along the pinned edge.** Notch the seam allowances along the curves, being careful not to clip through the stitching. Finger-press the seam allowances open.

4. **Repeat steps 1–3** to sew the lining bottom to the assembled lining front/back, leaving a 6" opening along a straight portion of the seam for turning.

5. **Turn the bag right side out.** Stitch the opening in the lining closed by hand or machine. Tuck the lining into the bag.

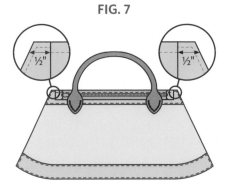

FIG. 7

½" ½"

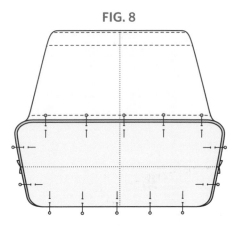

FIG. 8

Jump-Start Duffel

When you're on the go, go in style with a duffel featuring your favorite large-scale print. This roomy bag can double as a workout bag and travel carry-on. Multiple zippered pockets on the exterior create plenty of space to keep essentials within easy reach, and you can carry it by the handles or by its longer adjustable strap.

FINISHED SIZE: 19" x 9" x 8"

MATERIALS

Yardage is based on 42"-wide fabric unless otherwise noted.

1⅛ yards of purple solid for strap, strap extenders, handles, handle extenders, and pockets

1 yard of purple print for exterior*

1⅛ yards of dark-purple print for lining**

⅝ yard of 58"-wide Soft and Stable (or Thermolam Plus fusible fleece)

3⅛ yards of 20"-wide Shape-Flex fusible woven interfacing (or other medium-weight fusible interfacing)

1 package (3 yards) of ½"-wide "extra-wide" double-fold bias tape (or make your own)**

1 zipper, 16" long

4 zippers, 9" long

4 metal O-rings (1½")

1 metal rectangular ring (1½")

1 metal slider (1½")

2 rectangles, 9" x 18", of template plastic, ultra-firm interfacing (Peltex), or cardboard

A little extra fabric is allowed for cutting a large-scale directional print.

**If you prefer to make your own binding, purchase 1⅜ yards of the lining fabric and cut bias strips 2" wide, enough to total 80" when joined together, in addition to the pieces listed at right.*

CUTTING

The pattern for the end panel is on pattern sheet 2.

From the purple print, cut:
2 rectangles, 17⅝" x 20", for bag front and back
2 end panels, *on fold*

From the purple solid, cut:
1 rectangle, 5" x 42", for strap
2 rectangles, 5" x 30", for handles
4 rectangles, 5" x 14", for handle extenders
2 rectangles, 10" x 15", for side pockets
2 rectangles, 7" x 15", for end pockets
1 square, 5" x 5", for strap extender

From the dark-purple print, cut:
2 rectangles, 17⅝" x 20", for lining front and back
2 end panels, *on fold,* for lining end panels
2 rectangles, 9" x 18", for bottom stiffener

From the Soft and Stable, cut:
2 rectangles, 17⅝" x 20", for bag front and back
2 end panels, *on fold**

From the Shape-Flex, cut:
2 rectangles, 17⅝" x 20", for lining front and back
2 end panels, *on fold,* for lining end panels
1 rectangle, 5" x 42", for strap
2 rectangles, 5" x 30", for handles
4 rectangles, 5" x 14", for handle extenders
1 square, 5" x 5", for strap extender

Because the Soft and Stable is thick, you'll be able to cut more accurately if you prepare a full pattern from a folded piece of paper and use it to cut the stabilizer in a single layer without folding. You can also use the cut fabric, unfolded, as your pattern.

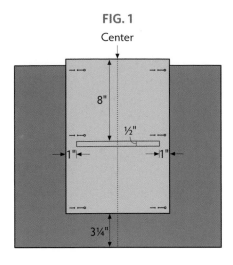

FIG. 1
Center

8"

½"

1" | 1"

3¼"

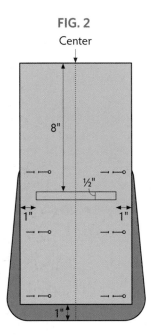

FIG. 2
Center

8"

½"

1" | 1"

1"

ATTACH THE INTERFACING

1. **Place the wrong side of the bag front** against the corresponding piece of Soft and Stable and pin. Baste ⅛" from the edges. Repeat to baste Soft and Stable to the bag back and end panels.

2. **Following the manufacturer's instructions,** fuse the Shape-Flex pieces to the wrong side of the strap, strap extender, handles, handle extenders, and lining front, back, and end panels.

ATTACH THE ZIPPERED POCKETS

All seam allowances are ½" unless otherwise noted.

1. **On the wrong side of one side pocket,** measure and mark a horizontal line 8" below one short edge. Draw a second horizontal line ½" below the first.

2. **Draw vertical lines** 1" from both side edges, connecting the horizontal lines to create a rectangular box.

3. **Finger-press the bag front and the side pocket** to find their vertical centerlines; the 20" edges are the top and bottom of the bag front. Pin the pocket to the bag front, right sides together, with the bottom of the pocket 3¼" above the bottom raw edge of the bag front and the centerlines matched (**fig. 1**).

4. **Following the instructions in "Zippered Pocket"** on page 86, make the zippered pocket in the bag front, using a 9"-long zipper. Repeat with the second side pocket and the bag back.

5. **Repeat steps 1–4** to attach an end pocket to each end panel. Position the pocket with its bottom edge 1" above the bottom raw edge of the end panel (**fig. 2**).

ATTACH THE TOP ZIPPER

1. **Sew the bag front and back together** at the top edge and press the seam allowances open. Repeat to join the lining front and back.

2. **On the wrong side of the lining,** draw lines ¼" from the seam on both sides (at the edges of the seam allowances). Draw vertical lines 2¼" from each side edge, connecting the previous lines to make a long rectangular box with the seam at its center.

3. **Position the lining on the bag body,** right sides together, aligning the seams. Pin the pieces together; your aim is to keep the seams aligned as you sew the zipper opening.

4. **Following the instructions in "Zippered Pocket,"** insert the 16"-long zipper. The lining takes the place of a pocket rectangle. After the rectangular opening is sewn and turned, smooth the lining over the wrong side of the bag body and match the raw edges before inserting the zipper.

ASSEMBLE THE STRAPS AND HANDLES

1. **Fold the strap in half lengthwise** with wrong sides together and press. Open the fold and press both long edges to the wrong side so that they meet at the center crease. Refold along the original crease and press once more. Topstitch ⅛" from each long edge. Repeat to make the strap extender, handles, and handle extenders.

2. **Slide the rectangular ring onto the strap extender.** Fold the extender in half, matching the raw edges. Pin the strap extender to the top edge of one end panel, centering it with the raw edges matched. Baste ¼" from the raw edge (**fig. 3**).

3. **Center one end of the strap** on the top edge of the second end panel, right sides together and raw edges matched. Baste ¼" from the raw edges.

4. **Pin the strap to the bag end** for now to keep it out of the way. Roll up the lining front and back individually and pin them near the zipper so you don't sew through the lining while attaching the handles.

5. **With a removable marking tool,** draw vertical lines on the bag front and back, 5" from each side edge.

6. **Press 1" to the wrong side** at one end of each handle extender. Slide an O-ring onto each handle extender, positioning it in the crease.

7. **Position a handle extender** along one of the lines from step 5, right side up, with the extender just inside the line and the raw edges aligned at the bottom. Be sure the pocket is smoothed into position against the wrong side of the bag, and that the lining is folded out of the way. Topstitch directly on top of the previous stitches, beginning at the bottom edge. When you near the O-ring, pivot and sew across the handle extender as close to the O-ring as possible. Pivot again and sew on the previous stitches to the bottom edge. **✱See "Zipper Caution," right.** Repeat to attach the other three handle extenders to the bag front and back (**fig. 4**).

8. **Press ½" to the wrong side** on each end of both handles. Press an additional 1" to the wrong side on each end.

9. **Thread one end of a handle** from front to back through the left O-ring on the bag front, setting the ring into the second pressed crease. Sew a small rectangle through all layers of the handle near the first fold, enclosing the raw edge. Slide the other end of the same handle into the right O-ring on the bag front and stitch in the same way. Repeat to attach the remaining handle to the bag back.

FIG. 3

Baste.

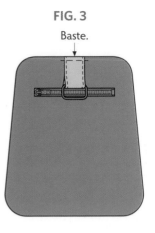

✱ *zipper caution*

The handle extenders will be sewn across the ends of the pocket zippers. Sew carefully and slowly (turn the machine flywheel by hand, if necessary), avoiding the metal zipper stops.

FIG. 4

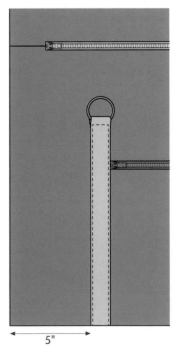

5"

There are lots of thick layers to stitch through in the final steps. Take a deep breath and sew slowly. Switch to a size 100/16 jeans/denim needle, which has a sharp point for piercing multiple layers of woven fabric and allows space to draw the thread through all those layers.

To be honest, binding the seam allowances requires the most patience of the whole project. Don't worry if your result isn't perfect; when the bag is turned right side out, the binding will be recessed into the corners of the bag and practically invisible.

* getting the bias straight

As you pin, gently stretch the bias tape to prevent ripples and puckers. If you're a quilter, you may prefer to sew and flip the binding as on a quilt, finishing its second edge by hand. One of my pattern testers recommends using ¼"-wide fusible-web tape to hold the binding in place for sewing.

FINISH THE BAG

1. **Sew the bag front and back together** along the bottom edge, keeping the lining pieces out of the way. Press the seam allowances open. Unpin the lining and sew the lining back and front together along the bottom edge. Press the seam allowances open. Unzip the zipper.

2. **Smooth the lining into place over the bag,** wrong sides together, so the bag body is wrong side out. Baste the lining to the bag body along the side edges, stitching ¼" from the raw edges.

3. **Place an end panel on a lining end panel,** wrong sides together, and baste ¼" from the raw edges. Make two.

4. **Find and mark the top and bottom centers** of the end panels. Pin an end panel to one side of the bag body, right sides together, matching the top and bottom seams to the center marks and distributing the fabric evenly around the curves. Be sure the handles and strap are tucked inside the bag. Sew the end panel to the bag body. Repeat to attach the remaining end panel to the other side of the bag body. ✻ See "Sewing Secrets," left.

5. **Cut two pieces of bias tape 40" long.** Fully unfold one end of each strip, press the unfolded end to the wrong side at a 45° angle, and fold the tape back into place.

6. **Beginning with the pressed end** at a straight part of the seam, slip the seam allowances of one end panel into one piece of bias tape. Be sure the raw edges are against the tape's center fold. Pin the tape over the seam allowances around the entire end panel. When you return to the beginning point, trim the excess tape, leaving a 1" overlap. Slide 1" of the bias tape inside the pressed tape end so that the raw edge of the tape is enclosed. Topstitch near the folded edge of the binding, sewing through all layers, to finish the seam allowances. Use the second piece of bias tape to finish the seam allowances around the other end panel. ✻ See "Getting the Bias Straight," left.

7. **Turn the bag right side out** and press well. Fold the bag, wrong sides together, along one seam at a time and press with steam. You may also use a wooden clapper to flatten the seams.

8. **Unpin the unfinished end of the strap** and weave it through the slider, passing over the slider's center bar. Thread the strap through the rectangular ring from the outside in, and then pass it over the slider's center bar again, under the other part of the strap. See "Metal Slider for an Adjustable Strap" on page 91 for more information.

9. **Press ½" to the wrong side** on the end of the strap. Fold an additional 3½" of the strap end to the wrong side, positioning the slider bar in the fold. Stitch a small rectangle through the strap near the first fold to secure the end around the slider bar. Don't sew through the first layer of the strap threaded through the slider. Refer to "Metal Slider for an Adjustable Strap" on page 91 for further instructions.

10. **Sew the two bottom-stiffener rectangles together** on three sides with a ¼" seam allowance, leaving one short edge open. Clip the sewn corners, turn the piece right side out, and press, turning ½" to the wrong side along the open edge.

11. **Slide the two pieces of stiffener** (cardboard, template plastic, or ultra-firm interfacing) into the opening. Topstitch ⅛" from the open end to close the opening and hold the stiffener in place. Place the stiffener in the bottom of your finished bag.

Sara says

This roomy duffel makes a great weekender bag, and a bold print makes it easy to spot in a sea of luggage!

Festival

Even if you prefer to carry a small bag, you can still make a big impact with a large-scale print. This small rounded bag, perfect for an outing to a music festival or a night on the town, is a standout with a twist lock on the flap, topstitched pockets in the lining, and graceful curves.

FINISHED SIZE: 11" x 7" x 3½"

MATERIALS

Yardage is based on 42"-wide fabric unless otherwise noted. Fat quarters measure approximately 18" x 21".

⅝ yard of large-scale print for exterior

¾ yard of pink print for lining

1 fat quarter of pink solid for piping and tabs

½ yard of 58"-wide Soft and Stable (or Thermolam Plus fusible fleece)

1¼ yards of 20"-wide Shape-Flex fusible woven interfacing (or other medium-weight fusible interfacing)

1 metal twist lock

2 metal rectangular rings (1½")

1½ yards of ⁵⁄₃₂"-diameter cotton cording

Optional: Wonder Under paper-backed fusible-web tape for assembling the piping

CUTTING

The patterns for the main panel/lining pocket, flap, and tab are on pattern sheet 2.

From the large-scale print, cut:
1 rectangle, 5" x 42", for strap
1 rectangle, 4½" x 24", for bag side/bottom
2 main panels, *on fold,* for bag front and back
1 flap, *on fold*

From the pink print, cut:
1 rectangle, 4½" x 24", for lining side/bottom
2 main panels, *on fold,* for lining front and back
4 lining pockets, *on fold;* shorten the main-panel pattern as indicated before cutting
1 flap, *on fold,* for flap lining

From the pink solid, cut:
4 tabs
1½"-wide bias strips, enough to total at least 48" when joined

From the Soft and Stable, cut:
1 rectangle, 4½" x 24", for bag side/bottom
2 main panels, *on fold,* for bag front and back*
1 flap, *on fold**

From the Shape-Flex, cut:
1 rectangle, 5" x 42", for strap
1 rectangle, 4½" x 24", for lining side/bottom
2 main panels, *on fold,* for lining front and back
1 flap, *on fold,* for lining flap
4 tabs

*Because the Soft and Stable is thick, you'll be able to cut more accurately if you prepare a full pattern from a folded piece of paper and use it to cut the stabilizer in a single layer without folding. You can also use the cut fabric, unfolded, as your pattern.

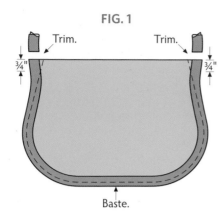

FIG. 1

Trim.   Trim.

¾"   ¾"

Baste.

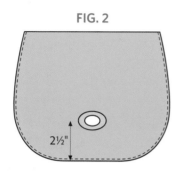

FIG. 2

2½"

* all locked up

Before installing a twist lock, examine it carefully. There are several different kinds available; some attach with screws and others use prongs.

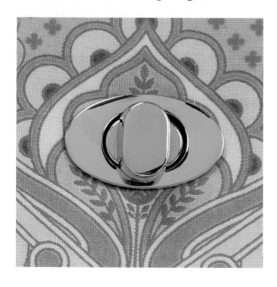

ATTACH THE INTERFACING

1. **Place the wrong side** of the bag side/bottom against the corresponding piece of Soft and Stable and pin. Baste ⅛" from the edges. Repeat to baste Soft and Stable to the bag front, back, and flap.

2. **Following the manufacturer's instructions,** fuse the Shape-Flex pieces to the wrong side of the strap, tabs, and lining side/bottom, front, back, and flap.

MAKE AND ATTACH THE PIPING

All seam allowances are ½" unless otherwise noted.

1. **Sew the bias strips together** end to end, and then cut two pieces, each 24" long. Also cut two 24"-long pieces of cording.

2. **Make two 24" lengths of piping** as directed in "Piping" on page 91. To baste the fabric around the cording, either stitch through the fabric close to the cording or use strips of paper-backed fusible web to adhere the fabric layers together.

3. **Pin one length of piping** to the sides and lower edge of the bag front, right sides together, matching the raw edges and easing the piping around the corner curves. Bend the ends of the piping outward slightly so that the cording tapers into the seamline about ¾" below the upper raw edge of the bag. Baste the piping to the bag front ¼" from the raw edges and trim the excess piping. Repeat to baste the second length of piping to the bag back (fig. 1).

ASSEMBLE THE FLAP AND LOCK

1. **With right sides together,** sew the flap and flap lining along the sides and lower edge, using a ¼" seam allowance. Leave the straight edge open. Notch the seam allowances along the curves, being careful not to clip through the stitching. Turn the flap right side out and press it flat.

2. **Topstitch ⅛"** from the sewn edges of the flap.

3. **Mark the location for the twist lock,** centered 2½" above the bottom of the flap. Following the manufacturer's instructions and the information in "Twist Locks" on page 93, install the opening for the twist lock on the flap (fig. 2). **✷ See "All Locked Up," left.**

4. **Mark the twist-lock location** on the bag front, centered 2½" from the top edge. Install the lock at the mark.

Sara says

Take the time to carefully center any large motifs when cutting the bag front and flap. You'll be glad you did!

MAKE THE LINING POCKETS

1. **With right sides together,** sew two lining pockets together along the top edge using a ¼" seam allowance. Turn the pocket right side out, matching the raw edges, and press it flat. Topstitch ⅛" from the finished edge. Make two.

2. **Place an assembled pocket** on the right side of the lining back, matching the raw edges. Baste ⅛" from the raw edges. Mark a line on the pocket 6" from the left edge. Topstitch along the line from the top edge of the pocket to the bottom raw edges, dividing the pocket into two sections.

3. **Repeat step 2** to add the second pocket to the lining front (fig. 3).

ATTACH THE TABS

1. **Fold the bag side/bottom in half,** matching the short ends. Mark the short ends ¾" from each side. Mark each side, 6" below the short ends. Draw diagonal lines connecting the marks on each side. Cut along the lines through both layers to shape the ends of the bag bottom; discard the scraps. Baste the fabric to the stabilizer ⅛" from each of the newly cut edges. Using the bag side/bottom as a guide, trim the lining side/bottom (fig. 4).

FIG. 3

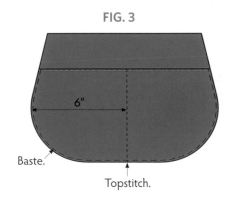

6"

Baste.

Topstitch.

FIG. 4

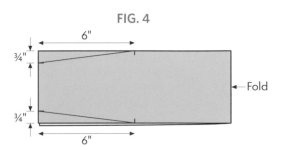

6"

¾"

¾"

6"

Fold

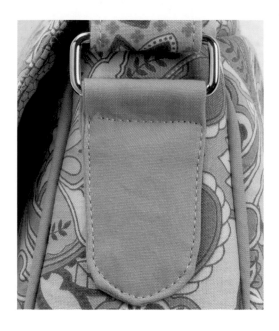

FIG. 5

1½"

Topstitch.

clipping right along

After pinning the bag sides to the bottom, I like to make ¼"-deep clips into the seam allowances along the curves to make easing the extra fabric into place easier.

FIG. 6

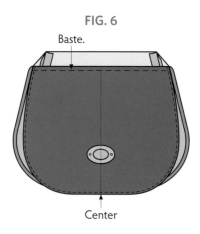

Baste.

Center

2. **Sew two tabs right sides together** using a ¼" seam allowance. Leave the short straight edge open. Notch the seam allowances along the curve. Turn the tab right side out and press it flat. Make two.

3. **Press 1" to the wrong side** on the unfinished end of one tab. Slide a rectangular ring onto the tab so that it rests in the crease. Repeat with the second tab and ring.

4. **Mark both short ends** of the bag side/bottom, 1½" below the top raw edge and centered from side to side. Place an assembled tab at one mark with the tab's raw edges between the tab and bag side. Pin in place.

5. **Topstitch ⅛" from the curved tab edge,** pivoting to stitch horizontally across the tab ¼" below the ring. Use a zipper foot if necessary. These stitches will secure the tab's raw edges underneath (fig. 5).

6. **Repeat steps 4 and 5** to attach the remaining tab to the opposite end of the bag.

ASSEMBLE THE BAG

1. **Fold the bag front, back, and side/bottom** to find and mark the bottom center of each piece.

2. **Pin the bag side/bottom** to the curved edge of the bag front, matching the bottom centers and upper raw edges and easing as necessary. ✳ **See "Clipping Right Along," left.**

3. **Sew the bag side/bottom** to the front. Notch the seam allowances along the curves, being careful not to cut into the stitching.

4. **Repeat steps 2 and 3** to attach the bag back to the other long edge of the bag side/bottom.

5. **Finger-press the bag back and the flap** to find the centers of their raw edges. Matching the centers and raw edges, pin the flap to the bag back with right sides together. Baste ¼" from the raw edges (fig. 6).

6. **Repeat steps 1–4** to assemble the lining, leaving a 6" opening in one seam along the bottom of the bag.

7. **Turn the bag exterior right side out.** Slip the lining over the exterior, right sides together, aligning the seams. Be sure that the flap and tabs are tucked inside, between the layers. Pin the lining to the bag along the top edge and then stitch.

8. **Turn the bag right side out** through the opening in the lining. Press the top edge, folding the flap away from the bag. Topstitch ¼" from the top seam, keeping the flap away from the topstitching.

9. **Close the opening** in the lining by hand or machine.

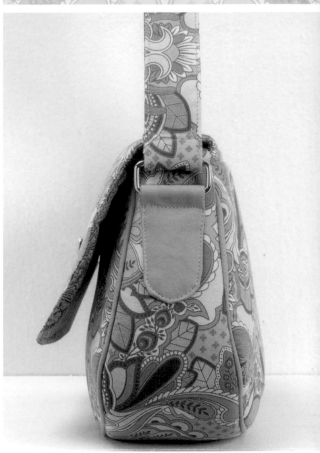

MAKE THE STRAP

1. **Press the strap in half lengthwise,** wrong sides together. Open the fold and press both long edges to the wrong side so that they meet at the center crease. Refold along the original crease and press once more. Topstitch ⅛" from both long edges.

2. **Press ½" to the wrong side** on each short end of the strap. Press an additional 1" to the wrong side on each end.

3. **Slide one end of the strap** through the rectangular ring on one side of the bag from the outside in, positioning the ring in the second crease. Sew a small rectangle through all layers of the strap near the ring, enclosing the raw edge and securing the ring. Repeat to attach the other end of the strap to the second rectangular ring. ✳ **See "Length Check," right.**

✳ length check

Before sewing the second end of the strap to secure the ring, pin it into place and check the fit over your arm. If the strap is too long for your preference, unpin and adjust the end before stitching.

Moon and Stars

Three-dimensional pockets give the outside of this bag a totally original look. I combined the pockets with color accents along the exterior seams, adding visual interest. It's a cute cross-body style with an adjustable strap and lots of space for inner storage.

FINISHED SIZE: 16" x 12½" x 4½"

MATERIALS

Yardage is based on 42"-wide fabric unless otherwise noted.

1 yard of pink-and-purple print for exterior
1 yard of purple dot for lining
½ yard of purple solid for trim
½ yard of 58"-wide Soft and Stable (or Thermolam Plus fusible fleece)
2⅛ yards of 20"-wide Shape-Flex fusible woven interfacing (or other medium-weight fusible interfacing)
1 metal rectangular ring (1½")
1 metal slider (1½")
3 magnetic snaps (½")
2 zippers, 12" long
Optional: 4 metal purse feet

* turn it down

Low-contrast prints (sometimes referred to as "low volume") work best for this bag's exterior because the rows of piping break the print into smaller sections.

CUTTING

The patterns for the main panel, bottom, pocket, tab, and flap are on pattern sheet 3.

From the pink-and-purple print, cut:
2 strips, 15" x 42"; crosscut into 12 rectangles, 3¾" x 15", for exterior panels. Use the remainder of the second strip to cut:
  1 bottom, *on fold*
  2 flaps
  2 pockets

From the purple dot, cut:
2 main panels, *on fold,* for lining front and back
1 bottom, *on fold,* for lining bottom
2 flaps for flap linings
2 pockets for pocket linings
2 rectangles, 10" x 20", for zippered pockets

From the purple solid, cut:
1 rectangle, 5" x 42", for strap
2 tabs
4 rectangles, 1½" x 13⅜", for pocket gussets
2 rectangles, 2½" x 15", for top accents
10 rectangles, 1" x 15", for exterior accents

From the Soft and Stable, cut:
2 main panels, *on fold,* for bag front and back*
1 bottom, *on fold,* for bag bottom*
2 flaps for flap lining
2 pockets
2 squares, 1½" x 1½", for snap reinforcement

*Because the Soft and Stable is thick, you'll be able to cut more accurately if you prepare a full pattern from a folded piece of paper and use it to cut the stabilizer in a single layer without folding. You can also use the cut fabric, unfolded, as your pattern.

Continued on page 50

Continued from page 48

From the Shape-Flex, cut:
1 rectangle, 5" x 42", for strap
2 main panels, *on fold,* for lining front and back
1 bottom, *on fold,* for lining bottom
2 flaps
2 pockets for pocket linings
2 tabs
4 rectangles, 1½" x 13⅜", for pocket gussets
2 rectangles, 2½ " x 15", for top accents

PIECE THE EXTERIOR

1. **Press each exterior-accent rectangle** in half lengthwise, with wrong sides together.

2. **Place a folded exterior accent** on the right edge of an exterior panel, matching the raw edges, and baste ⅛" from the raw edges. Place a second exterior panel on the assembled unit, right sides together, with the accent strip between the panels. Sew, using a ¼" seam allowance. Open the panels and press the seam allowances to the right, pressing the accent strip to the left. Make a unit six panels wide, with five accent strips in the seams. Make two units **(fig. 1)**.

3. **Using the lining front as a pattern,** stack the pieced exteriors with the lining front on top and centered. Trim the pieced units to match the lining front; they will now be called the bag front and back.

ATTACH THE INTERFACING

1. **Place the wrong side of the bag front** against the corresponding piece of Soft and Stable and pin. Baste ⅛" from the edges. Repeat to baste Soft and Stable to the bag back and bottom, flap linings, and exterior pockets.

2. **Following the manufacturer's instructions,** fuse the Shape-Flex pieces to the wrong side of the strap; lining bottom, front, and back; flaps; pocket linings and gussets; tabs; and top accents.

FIG. 1

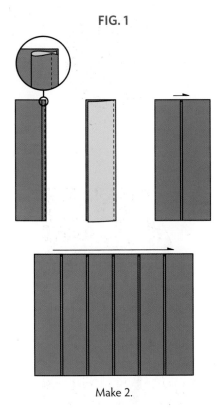

Make 2.

ASSEMBLE THE EXTERIOR POCKETS

All seam allowances are ½" unless otherwise noted.

1. **Measure and mark each pocket** 3¼" from the top edge and centered from side to side. Install the socket of a magnetic snap at each mark, following the manufacturer's instructions and the information in "Magnetic Snaps" on page 88.

2. **Measure and mark** each flap lining 1" above the curved lower edge and centered from side to side. Install the ball half of a magnetic snap at each mark.

3. **Sew a pocket lining** to a prepared pocket, right sides together, using a ¼" seam allowance and leaving a 4" opening along the straight top edge. Clip the corners and notch the seam allowances to reduce bulk, being careful not to clip through the stitching.

4. **Turn the pocket right side out.** Press the pocket flat, pressing the seam allowances along the opening to the wrong side. Topstitch ⅛" from the straight edge, closing the opening as you stitch. Make two pocket units.

5. **Repeat step 3** with a flap and flap lining. Turn the flap right side out and press it flat, pressing the seam allowances along the opening to the wrong side. Topstitch ⅛" from the curved side/bottom edge. Make two flap units.

6. **Sew two pocket gussets together** along all four sides with a ¼" seam allowance, leaving a 4" opening along one long edge. Clip the corners.

7. **Turn the gusset right side out.** Press the gusset flat, pressing the seam allowances to the wrong side along the opening. Make two pocket gussets. **✱ See "Turning Tip," right.**

8. **Pin a gusset to a pocket unit,** right sides together, matching the long edge of the gusset containing the opening to the pocket's curved edge and aligning the straight edges at the top of the pocket. (The edges are all finished at this point, eliminating raw edges inside the finished pocket.) Sew the gusset to the pocket using an ⅛" seam allowance and closing the opening in the gusset seam as you sew. Press the seam allowances toward the pocket. Make two **(fig. 2)**. **✱ See "Make It Ease-y," right.**

9. **Transfer the pocket locations** to the bag front from the main-panel pattern. Turn the pocket units right side out and pin one to the bag front at each marked location, with the free edge of the gusset along the placement line.

10. **Using a zipper foot,** sew the free edge of each gusset to the bag front, stitching ⅛" from the gusset edge. The gusset will stand at a right angle to the bag front, holding the pocket away from the bag **(fig. 3).**

✱ *turning tip*

Turning pieces right side out may seem tedious. Take your time and work slowly, gently pushing the end of the piece into the tube and then pulling it through the opening.

✱ *make it ease-y*

I recommend sewing both sides of the pocket/gusset seam first, then sewing the bottom and curved corners. This stitching order makes it simpler to ease in extra fabric around the curves.

FIG. 2

⅛"

Make 2.

FIG. 3

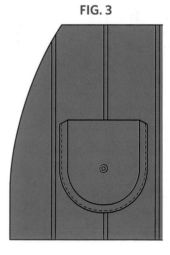

FIG. 4

Topstitch.

FIG. 5

Trim.   Trim.

11. **Lay an assembled flap on the bag front,** right sides together, with the straight edge of the flap abutting the top of the pocket. The snap/lining side of the flap will face upward, with the curve of the flap toward the top of the bag. Topstitch ⅛" and ¼" from the straight edge of the flap. Fold the flap downward to fasten the magnetic snap. Repeat to attach the second flap above the second pocket **(fig. 4).**

ASSEMBLE THE EXTERIOR

1. **Press ¼" to the wrong side** along the bottom edge of each top-accent rectangle.

2. **Align the long raw edge** of the top accent with the top edge of the bag front, right sides facing up, and pin. Topstitch ⅛" from the pressed edge through all thicknesses. Trim the accent rectangle to match the curves of the bag front at the side edges. Repeat to attach the second accent rectangle to the bag back **(fig. 5).**

3. **Sew the bag front** to the bag back at the sides, aligning the edges of the top accents. Notch the seam allowances along the curves and press them open.

4. *Optional:* Transfer the purse-feet placements from the bottom pattern to the bag bottom. Install the purse feet at the marks, following the manufacturer's instructions and the information in "Purse Feet" on page 89. ✳**See "Perfect Feet" on page 55.**

5. **Pin the bottom edge** of the assembled bag to the bottom, right sides together and raw edges matched, aligning the side seams with the notches. Ease the bag as necessary around the bottom curves.

6. **Sew along the pinned edge.** Notch the curved edges of the bag bottom to reduce bulk. Press the seam allowances open. **＊See "Super Curves," right.**

MAKE THE ZIPPERED POCKETS

1. **Draw a horizontal line** 11" below the top short edge of one zippered-pocket rectangle. Draw a second horizontal line ½" below the first.

2. **Draw vertical lines** 1" from the side edges, connecting the horizontal lines to form a rectangular box.

3. **Finger-press the lining front** and the pocket rectangle to find the vertical centerlines. Pin the pocket to the lining, right sides together, with the bottom edge of the pocket 1" above the bottom of the lining front and the centerlines matched **(fig. 6)**.

4. **Follow the instructions in "Zippered Pocket"** on page 86 to complete the lining pocket.

5. **Repeat steps 1–4** with the second pocket rectangle and the lining back.

ASSEMBLE THE LINING

1. **Measure and mark** the lining front 1½" below the top edge and centered from side to side. Install one half of the remaining magnetic snap at the mark, using a 1½" square of Soft and Stable to reinforce the opening. Repeat to attach the other half of the snap to the lining back.

2. **Sew the lining front and back together** at the sides. Press the seam allowances open, clipping the curves as necessary.

3. **Sew the assembled lining** to the lining bottom as you did for the bag-exterior pieces, but leave an 8" opening along one straight edge of the bag bottom for turning.

4. **Notch the seam allowances** along the curves. Press the seam allowances to the wrong side along the opening.

＊ super curves

It's important to sew smooth, even curves around the bag bottom, so take your time. Sew slowly and reduce the stitch length to 12 to 14 stitches per inch if necessary to maintain a consistent seam allowance.

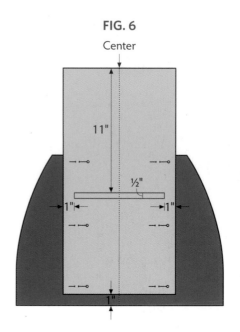

FIG. 6

Center

11"

½"

1"

1"

1"

Thanks to the metal slider, you can adjust the strap to wear the bag either over your shoulder or across you body. How convenient!

ATTACH THE STRAP

1. **Sew the tabs together** along the curved edge using a ¼" seam allowance. Leave the short straight edge open. Notch the seam allowances along the curves. Turn the tab right side out, and press it flat.

2. **Press 2" of the curved tab end** to the wrong side. Slide the rectangular ring onto the tab so it lies in the crease.

3. **Sew across the folded tab** ¼" from the ring. Pivot and continue stitching along the curved end of the tab, ⅛" from the edge, until you return to the straight line of stitches. Overlap the ends of the stitching slightly and backstitch to secure.

4. **Center the tab** over the left side seam of the bag exterior, right sides together and raw edges matched. The curved end of the tab will lie against the bag. Baste ¼" from the raw edges (fig. 7).

5. **Fold the strap in half lengthwise** with wrong sides together and press. Open the strap and press the long edges to the wrong side so that they meet at the crease. Refold along the original crease and press again. Topstitch ⅛" from both long edges.

6. **Center one end** of the strap over the bag's right side seam, right sides together and raw edges matched. Baste ¼" from the raw edges.

7. **Slide the loose end of the strap** through the slider, weaving it over the slider's center bar. Thread the end of the strap through the rectangular ring on the tab from right side to wrong side. See "Metal Slider for an Adjustable Strap" on page 91 for more information.

8. **Weave the strap end** through the slider once more, underneath the first pass of the strap. Fold ½" to the wrong side on the end of the strap and sew the folded end to the bottom layer of the strap near the slider, enclosing the raw edges and securing the slider. The topstitching should form a small rectangle to fully secure the strap. Refer to "Metal Slider for an Adjustable Strap" for further instructions.

FIG. 7

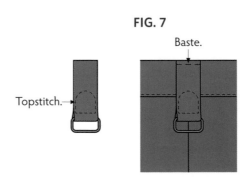

Topstitch. Baste.

FINISH THE BAG

1. **Slide the lining over the bag** so that they are right sides together. Align the top edges and match the side seams. Make sure that the strap is tucked between the fabric layers, away from the top edge. Stitch the top edge of the bag.

2. **Turn the bag right side out** through the opening in the lining. Tuck the lining into the bag and press the top seam flat. Topstitch ⅛" from the top edge of the bag.

3. **Close the opening** in the lining by hand or machine.

* perfect feet

Use a drop of seam sealant to prevent fraying when you cut the slits for purse feet.

Trompe le Monde

The wide-open front and back panels of this fancy tote bag are perfect for a striking large-scale print, such as the 13"-tall witch cameo by Tula Pink shown here. The thumb-catch hardware makes this easy-to-open bag practical enough for everyday use.

FINISHED SIZE: 12½" x 13½" x 5"

MATERIALS

Yardage is based on 42"-wide fabric unless otherwise noted.

¾ yard of purple print for exterior*

1 yard of blue print #1 for lining

½ yard of blue print #2 for divider pocket

½ yard of gray print for divider-pocket lining

⅔ yard of black solid for the straps, piping, and trim

⅝ yard of 58"-wide Soft and Stable (or Thermolam Plus fusible fleece)

3⅝ yards of 20"-wide Shape-Flex fusible woven interfacing (or other medium-weight fusible interfacing)

1 metal thumb catch

4 metal rectangular rings (1½")

1 zipper, 12" long

2¾ yards of ⁵⁄₃₂"-diameter cotton cording

Optional: Wonder Under paper-backed fusible-web tape for assembling the piping

You may need to purchase more fabric if you are fussy cutting a large print.

CUTTING

The patterns for the main panel/lining pocket, side accent, flap, and tab are on pattern sheet 3.

From the purple print, cut:

1 rectangle, 6" x 42", for bag side/bottom

2 main panels, *on fold,* for bag front and back

From blue print #1, cut:

2 rectangles, 3½" x 42", for lining side/bottom

2 main panels, *on fold,* for lining front and back

2 lining pockets, *on fold;* shorten the main-panel pattern as indicated before cutting

From blue print #2, cut:

2 main panels, *on fold,* for divider pocket; trim 1½" from the straight top edge of each piece

2 rectangles, 1½" x 3", for zipper tabs

From the gray print, cut:

2 main panels, *on fold,* for divider-pocket lining; trim 1½" from the straight top edge of each piece

From the black solid, cut:

2 rectangles, 5" x 36", for straps

4 side accents

2 flaps

8 tabs

1½"-wide bias strips, enough to total at least 84" when joined.

From the Soft and Stable, cut:

1 rectangle, 6" x 42", for bag side/bottom

2 main panels, *on fold,* for bag front and back**

From the Shape-Flex, cut:

2 rectangles, 3½" x 42", for lining side/bottom

6 main panels, *on fold,* for lining front and back and divider pocket; trim 1½" from the straight top edge of four pieces for the divider pocket

2 rectangles, 5" x 36", for straps

2 flaps

8 tabs

**Because the Soft and Stable is thick, you'll be able to cut more accurately if you prepare a full pattern from a folded piece of paper and use it to cut the stabilizer in a single layer without folding. You can also use the cut fabric, unfolded, as your pattern.*

FIG. 1

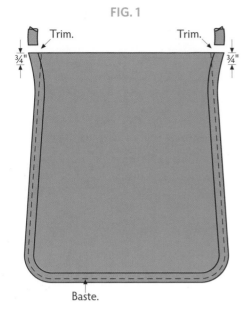

Trim.   Trim.

¾"   ¾"

Baste.

FIG. 2

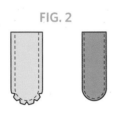

---

* thumb-catch pointers

The catch in the sample bag is attached with two screws; yours may be different, so be sure to check the manufacturer's instructions.

To position the catch correctly, begin by marking the center of the flap's curved end. Center the thumb catch over the mark and use it as a template to mark the locations of the screws.

Use an awl or tiny hole punch to pierce the flap at the marks; then replace the thumb catch and secure the screws.

ATTACH THE INTERFACING

1. **Place the wrong side of the bag front** against the corresponding piece of Soft and Stable and pin. Baste ⅛" from the edges. Repeat to baste Soft and Stable to the bag back and side/bottom.

2. **Following the manufacturer's instructions,** fuse the Shape-Flex pieces to the wrong side of the lining side/bottom, front, and back; divider pocket; straps; flaps; and tabs.

MAKE AND ATTACH THE PIPING

All seam allowances are ½" unless otherwise noted.

1. **Sew the bias strips together** end to end, and then cut the strip into two pieces, 42" long. Also cut two 42"-long pieces of cording. Make two lengths of piping as directed in "Piping" on page 91. To baste the fabric around the cording, either stitch through the fabric close to the cording or use strips of paper-backed fusible web to adhere the fabric layers together.

2. **Pin one length of piping** to the side and bottom edges of the bag front, easing the piping around the corner curves. Beginning ¾" below the top edge of the bag front, curve the ends of the piping toward the raw edges so that they taper into the seamline. Baste the piping to the bag front ¼" from the raw edges. Trim the excess piping (fig. 1).

3. **Repeat step 2** to baste the remaining length of piping to the bag back.

ASSEMBLE THE FLAP

1. **Sew the flap pieces together** along the curved edge using a ¼" seam allowance. Leave the short straight end open. Notch the seam allowances along the curves, being careful not to clip through the stitching. Turn the flap right side out and press it flat. Topstitch ⅛" from the finished edge (fig. 2).

2. **Following the manufacturer's instructions,** install the male half of the thumb catch at the center of the flap's short curved edge. ✱**See "Thumb-Catch Pointers," left.**

3. **Find and mark the centers of the bag back** and the flap raw edge. Place the flap on the bag back, right sides together (the right side of the catch will be against the bag's right side), matching the raw edges and centers. Baste ¼" from the raw edges.

4. **Measure and mark the bag front** 2¾" below the top edge and centered from side to side. Install the female half of the thumb catch at the mark.

MAKE AND ATTACH THE STRAPS

1. **Fold one strap in half lengthwise,** wrong sides together, and press. Open the fold and press both long edges to the wrong side so that they meet at the center crease. Refold along the original crease and press once more. Topstitch ⅛" from both long edges. Make two.

2. **Sew two tab pieces together** along the curved edge using a ¼" seam allowance. Leave the short straight edge open. Notch the seam allowances along the curve. Turn the tab right side out. Press the tab flat. Make four.

3. **Press 1" of the tab's unfinished end** to the wrong side. Slide a rectangular ring onto the tab, resting it in the crease. Repeat with the remaining tabs and rings (fig. 3).

4. **Transfer the tab placement marks** from the main-panel pattern to the bag front and back. ***See "Easy Marking," below right.**

5. **Place an assembled tab** within the placement mark on one side of the bag front, with the pressed end of the tab between the bag front and tab. Pin the tab to the bag.

6. **Topstitch ⅛" from the curved tab edge.** When you near the rectangular ring, pivot and sew horizontally across the tab ¼" below the ring. Pivot again to finish, overlapping a few stitches and backstitching to secure the ring. Use a zipper foot for stitching close to the rectangular ring.

7. **Repeat steps 5 and 6** to attach a second tab and ring to the other side of the bag front and the final two tabs with rings to the bag back.

8. **Press ½" to the wrong side** on each end of both straps. Press an additional 1" to the wrong side on each end.

9. **Slide one strap end through a rectangular ring** on the bag front from front to back, resting the ring in the second crease. Sew a small rectangle through the strap end near the first fold, enclosing the raw edges. Thread the other end of the same strap through the second ring on the bag front, making sure the strap isn't twisted, and pin the strap end. Test the strap length on your shoulder; if it's too long, unpin the end and adjust. Stitch the second end of the strap as before (fig. 4).

10. **Repeat step 9** to attach the remaining strap to the bag back. If you adjusted the strap length, be sure to make the same change to the second strap.

FIG. 3

Make 4.

* *easy marking*

I find it easiest to simply cut the tab area out of the paper pattern for the main panel to make a stencil for transferring the locations to the bag pieces.

FIG. 4

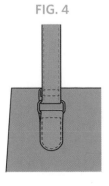

ASSEMBLE THE EXTERIOR

1. **Fold the bag side/bottom in half,** matching the short ends. Measure and mark the short ends 1" from each side edge. Measure and mark each side 12" from the short ends. Draw a diagonal line connecting the marks on each side and cut along the lines. Baste the fabric to the stabilizer ⅛" from each of the newly cut edges (fig. 5).

2. **Sew two side accent pieces together** along the curved edge using a ¼" seam allowance. Leave the short straight edge open. Notch the seam allowances along the curves. Turn the accent piece right side out, and press it flat. Make two.

3. **Center an assembled side accent** along one top edge of the side/bottom, right sides up, matching the raw edges at the short end. Pin in place. Topstitch ⅛" from the finished edge of the accent piece. Repeat to attach the second side accent to the other top edge of the side/bottom (fig. 6).

4. **Finger-press the bag front and back** to find and mark their vertical centers; fold the side/bottom in half widthwise and mark the bottom center. Pin one long raw edge of the side/bottom to the sides and bottom edge of the bag front, matching the centers and easing the fabric around the corner curves. Sew along the pinned edge (fig. 7).

5. **Repeat step 4** to sew the bag back to the free edge of the side/bottom.

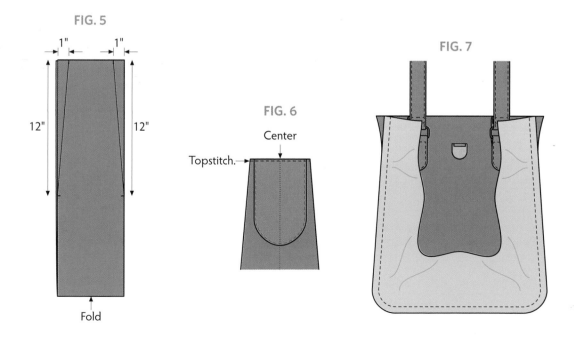

FIG. 5

1" 1"

12" 12"

Fold

FIG. 6

Center

Topstitch

FIG. 7

ASSEMBLE THE LINING

1. **Sew the lining pockets together** along the top edge using a ¼" seam allowance. Turn the pocket right side out, matching the raw edges, and press. Topstitch ⅛" from the finished edge.

2. **Pin the lining pocket to the lining back,** right sides up, with the raw edges aligned. Baste ⅛" from the raw edges. Measure and mark a vertical line 7" from the left edge. Topstitch along the line, dividing the pocket into two sections (fig. 8).

3. **Fold a zipper tab in half crosswise** with wrong sides together, matching the short edges, and press. Open the fold and press both short edges to the wrong side so the raw edges meet at the center crease. Refold along the original crease and press once more, enclosing the raw edges. Make two (fig. 9).

4. **Measure the zipper from the top edge** of the zipper tape and trim it exactly 11" long.

5. **Slide one end of the zipper into a zipper tab,** resting the end of the zipper against the tab's center crease, and pin. Topstitch ⅛" from the folded fabric edges to secure the zipper. Be sure to catch all the layers of the zipper tab in the seam, and stitch very carefully across the zipper (turning the flywheel by hand, if necessary) to avoid breaking a needle. Repeat to attach the second zipper tab to the other end of the zipper (fig. 10).

6. **Trim the raw edges of the zipper tabs** so that they are the same width as the zipper.

7. **Center the assembled zipper unit** on one divider pocket, right sides together, aligning the edge of the zipper tape with the pocket's top edge. The pocket will extend ½" beyond the zipper tab on each end. Using a zipper foot and a ¼" seam allowance, sew the assembled zipper unit to the divider pocket (fig. 11).

8. **Pin a divider-pocket lining** to the unit along the top edge, right sides together, sandwiching the zipper between the pockets. Sew directly on top of the stitching from the previous step. Turn the unit right side out, matching raw edges, and press it flat. Topstitch ⅛" from the seam.

9. **Repeat steps 7 and 8** to attach the other side of the zipper to the remaining divider-pocket pieces. Switch back to a regular sewing machine foot. Fold the pocket in half along the zipper, lining sides together, matching the raw edges. Baste the four layers together ⅛" from the raw edges.

FIG. 8

7"

Baste.

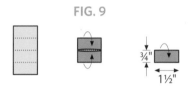

FIG. 9

¾"

1½"

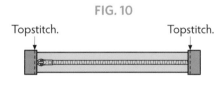

FIG. 10

Topstitch.   Topstitch.

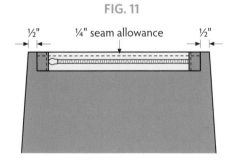

FIG. 11

½"   ¼" seam allowance   ½"

* keeping it straight

Sometimes it's hard to distinguish the gently tapered edge of the side/bottom from the one that's perfectly straight. Mark the tapered edges of both panels so that you can easily determine which is which.

* one at a time

You may find it easier to stitch the lining side panels to the divider pocket one at a time rather than pinning and sewing both at once.

* slow and steady

Sew slowly or even turn the handwheel manually as you near the top of the divider pocket. The fabric layers will be very thick there.

10. **Fold both lining side/bottoms in half,** matching the short edges. Arrange the two pieces side by side as shown. Measure and mark the short edge of the left panel 1" from its left edge; mark the right panel 1" from its right edge. Measure and mark the outer edges of both panels 12" below the short ends. Draw a diagonal line connecting the marks on each panel and cut along the lines. Measure and mark each inner (straight) edge 2½" below each short end (fig. 12). **✳ See "Keeping It Straight," left.**

11. **Finger-press the lining side/bottoms** and the divider pocket to find and mark the centers. Pin the straight edge of one side/bottom to the divider pocket, right sides together, matching the centers. Align the top of the pocket with the 2½" marks on the side/bottom and ease the excess fabric around the curved corners. Pin the straight edge of the second side/bottom to the unit, right sides together, with the divider pocket between the side/bottom panels. Continue pinning the side panels together above the pocket (fig. 13). **✳ See "One at a Time," left.**

12. **Sew along the pinned edge** to attach the lining side/bottoms to the divider pocket. Press the seam allowances open above the pocket. **✳ See "Slow and Steady," left.**

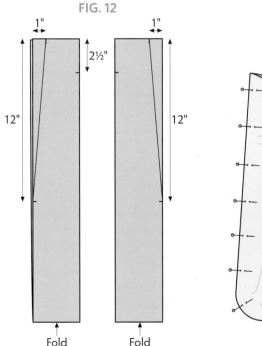

FIG. 12

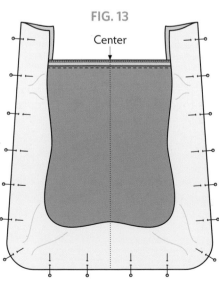

FIG. 13

Center

13. **Finger-press the lining front and back** to find and mark the vertical centerlines. Pin one long raw edge of the assembled lining side/bottom to the sides and bottom raw edge of the lining front, matching the centerlines and easing the excess fabric to fit around the curves. Sew along the pinned edge. **＊See "Ease-y Seaming," right.**

14. **Repeat step 13** to sew the remaining long edge of the lining side/bottom to the lining back, leaving an 8" opening along the bag bottom for turning.

FINISH THE BAG

1. **Turn the bag exterior right side out.** Slip the lining over the exterior, right sides together. Align the top edges and the side seams, and make sure that the flap and straps are tucked between the fabric layers. Pin around the top edge.

2. **Sew along the pinned edge.** Turn the bag right side out through the opening in the lining. Tuck the lining inside the bag and press the top edge flat, pressing the flap away from the bag. Topstitch ¼" from the top edge, keeping the tabs and flap away from the stitching.

3. **Close the opening in the lining** by hand or machine.

＊ ease-y seaming

To release the edges for easier sewing, make ¼"-long clips into the seam allowances along curves before you sew.

Copilot

One of my most popular published patterns is Aeroplane Bag, a large bag meant for travel. Now you can carry a purse-size Copilot version. The bottom of the bag is sturdy, the upper edge shaped by darts, and the top zipper very easy to install. And there's no hand sewing necessary!

FINISHED SIZE: 14½" x 12" x 5"

MATERIALS

Yardage is based on 42"-wide fabric unless otherwise noted.

⅜ yard of hexagon print for bag front and back*

¼ yard of blue solid for bag bottom*

¼ yard of white print for straps

1 yard of beige print for lining

⅜ yard of 58"-wide Soft and Stable (or Thermolam Plus fusible fleece)

2½ yards of 20"-wide Shape-Flex fusible woven interfacing (or other medium-weight fusible interfacing)

⅝ yard of Peltex ultra-firm interfacing (or other extra-heavy sew-in interfacing)

1 zipper, 20" long

1 zipper, 9" long

If your fabric has less than 42" of useable width, you'll need to purchase ¾ yard of the hexagon print and ⅜ yard of the blue solid.

CUTTING

The pattern for the main panel is on pattern sheet 4.

From the hexagon print, cut:
2 main panels, *on fold,* for bag front and back

From the blue solid, cut:
2 rectangles, 5" x 20½", for bag bottom

From the white print, cut:
2 rectangles, 4" x 42", for straps

From the beige print, cut:
1 rectangle, 10" x 20", for lining pocket
Reserve the remaining beige print for cutting the lining front and back.

From the Soft and Stable, cut:
2 main panels, *on fold,* for bag front and back*

From the Shape-Flex, cut:
2 rectangles, 4" x 42", for straps
2 rectangles, 5" x 20½", for bag bottom
Reserve the remaining Shape-Flex for cutting the lining front and back.

From the Peltex, cut:
2 rectangles, 4" x 19½", for bag bottom**

Because the Soft and Stable is thick, you'll be able to cut more accurately if you prepare a full pattern from a folded piece of paper and use it to cut the stabilizer in a single layer without folding. You can also use the cut fabric, unfolded, as your pattern.

**The Peltex rectangles are ½" smaller on each side than their fabric counterparts to reduce bulk in the seam allowance.*

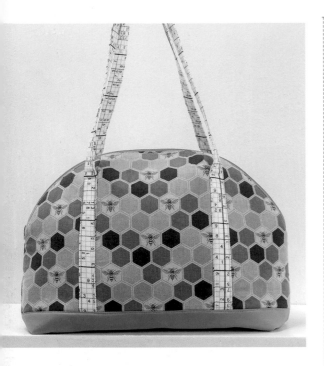

ATTACH THE INTERFACING

1. **Place the wrong side of the bag front** against the corresponding piece of Soft and Stable and pin. Baste ⅛" from the edges. Repeat to baste Soft and Stable to the bag back.

2. **Following the manufacturer's instructions,** fuse the Shape-Flex pieces to the wrong side of the straps.

3. **Center a Peltex rectangle** on the wrong side of one bag bottom. Cover the Peltex with a Shape-Flex rectangle, adhesive side down and raw edges matched. Following the manufacturer's instructions, fuse the Shape-Flex to the fabric and Peltex to hold the Peltex in place. Make two.

MAKE THE STRAPS

All seam allowances are ½" unless otherwise noted.

1. **Fold one strap in half lengthwise** with the wrong sides together and press. Open the fold and press both long edges to the wrong side so that they meet at the center crease. Refold along the original crease and press once more. Topstitch ⅛" from both long edges. Make two.

2. **Measure and mark the bag front** 6" from each side seam, drawing vertical lines across the bag front with a removable marking tool. Repeat to mark the bag back.

3. **Lay one end of a prepared strap** on the bag front just inside the left-hand line, with the raw edge of the strap aligned with the bottom edge of the bag front. Pin the strap to the bag. Position the other end of the strap just inside the right-hand line on the bag front, ensuring that the strap is not twisted, and pin. Draw a horizontal line across each strap 8" above the bottom of the bag front.

4. **Topstitch the strap ends to the bag front** by sewing over the existing topstitching. Begin sewing at the bottom of the bag; when you reach the horizontal line, pivot and stitch across the strap. Pivot again at the end of the line and sew to the bottom of the bag (fig. 1).

5. **Repeat steps 3 and 4** to attach the remaining strap to the bag back.

6. **Sew the lower edge of the bag front** to one long edge of a bag bottom. Press the seam allowances toward the bag bottom and topstitch the bottom ⅛" from the seam (fig. 2).

7. **Repeat step 6** to sew the bag back to the second bag bottom.

FIG. 1

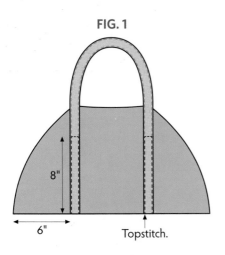

8"

6"

Topstitch.

FIG. 2

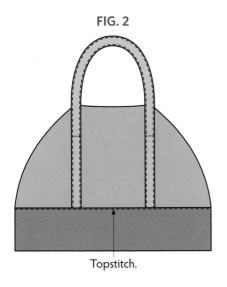

Topstitch.

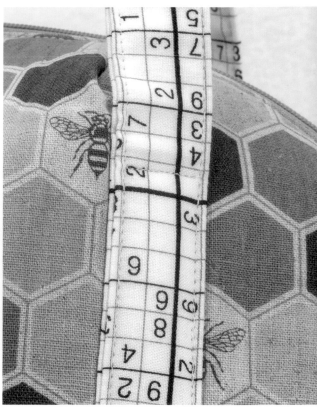

MAKE THE ZIPPERED POCKET

1. **Using the assembled bag front as a pattern,** trace and cut two pieces *each* from the beige print and Shape-Flex. Fuse one piece of Shape-Flex to each beige-print piece; these are the lining front and back.

2. **On the wrong side of the lining pocket,** measure and mark a horizontal line 10½" below the top short edge. Draw a second horizontal line ½" below the first.

3. **Draw vertical lines 1" from each side edge** of the pocket rectangle, connecting the horizontal lines and creating a narrow rectangular box.

4. **Finger-press the lining back and pocket** to find and mark their vertical centerlines. Pin the pocket to the lining back, right sides together, matching the centerlines, with the bottom edge of the pocket 1" above the bottom of the lining back (fig. 3).

5. **Following the instructions in "Zippered Pocket"** on page 86, sew the pocket to the lining back. Use the 9"-long zipper for the pocket opening.

FIG. 3

Center

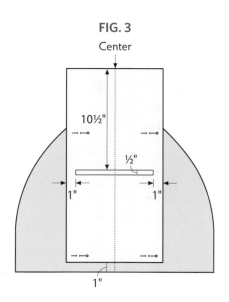

10½"

½"

1"   1"

1"

* magic marker

Punch a small hole in the paper pattern at the point of the dart. You'll be able to mark a dot through the hole onto the wrong side of the fabric. Then connect the point to the ends of the seamlines by tracing along a ruler.

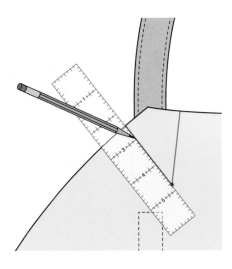

* finding your center

To align the zipper and bag at their centers, finger-press and mark the centers before positioning the zipper on the bag.

ATTACH THE TOP ZIPPER

1. **Transfer the dart markings** from the main-panel pattern to the wrong sides of the bag and lining fronts and backs. Be sure to mark the point of the dart as well as the ends of the dart seamlines. **＊See "Magic Marker," left.**

2. **Fold the bag front,** right sides together, matching the seamlines on the sides of one dart. Stitch the dart, sewing directly on the marked lines. Trim the excess fabric leaving ¼" seam allowances. Press the seam allowances open. Repeat to construct the remaining darts in the bag front and back and lining front and back **(fig. 4).**

3. **Center the zipper on the top edge** of the bag front, right sides together and edges matched; pin. Using a zipper foot and ¼" seam allowance, sew the 20"-long zipper to the bag front. Taper the ends of the zipper tapes into the seam allowance so they will not be visible in the finished bag **(fig. 5). ＊See "Finding Your Center," left.**

4. **Place the lining front on the bag front** with right sides together and top edges matched, sandwiching the zipper between fabric layers. Be sure the exterior and lining darts are aligned. Stitch again on top of the seam from step 3.

5. **Flip the fabrics open** so that the bag and lining fronts are wrong sides together. Press the fabrics flat along the zipper. Topstitch ⅛" from the seam along the zipper.

6. **Unzip the zipper.** Repeat steps 3–5 to attach the bag and lining backs to the other edge of the zipper tape. As you pin, be sure the darts are aligned across the zipper tape for a neat finished appearance.

FIG. 4

Trim.

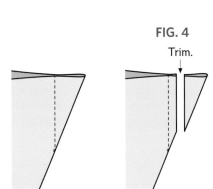

FIG. 5

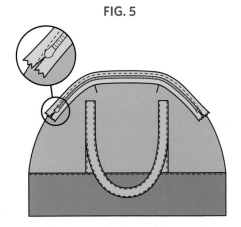

Don't be intimidated by darts! They're a quick and easy way to add shaping.

FINISH THE BAG

1. **With the zipper still unzipped,** separate the lining and exterior fabric layers. Match the bag front to the bag back (exterior pieces) with right sides together. Sew the sides and bottom edge, making sure the side seams extend to the end of the zipper stitching or overlap it slightly. The seam allowances are ½", but the side seams will taper to ¼" to match the zipper stitching.

2. **To box a lower corner of the bag,** refold the bag exterior so that one side seam is aligned with the bottom seam. Push a pin through the seamlines to be sure the side and bottom seams are aligned. Measure and mark a line perpendicular to the seams 2½" below the point, creating a triangle. Sew along the line through all the layers. Trim the seam allowances to ¼" and finger-press them open **(fig. 6).**

3. **Repeat step 2** to box the second corner of the bag exterior.

4. **Rearrange the bag** so that the lining back and front are right sides together with their raw edges matched. Repeat steps 1–3 to assemble the lining, using a ⅝" seam allowance below the zipper to help the lining fit inside the bag. Leave an 8" opening at the center of the bottom seam for turning.

5. **Turn the bag right side out** through the opening in the lining. Press the seam allowances along the opening to the wrong side and stitch the opening closed by hand or machine. Tuck the lining inside the bag and press well along the zipper for a neat finished appearance.

FIG. 6

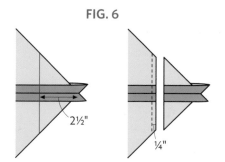

2½"

¼"

Beguiling

Beguiling is full of professional detailing, such as side panels and a top zipper, plus a flap closure that really makes a statement. Yet with all its beauty, it's still small enough to carry on your shoulder with a swing in your step . . . because you just made a gorgeous new bag for yourself!

FINISHED SIZE: 10" x 6½" x 3"

MATERIALS

Yardage is based on 42"-wide fabric unless otherwise noted.

½ yard of purple print for exterior

⅝ yard of gray print for lining

¼ yard of gray solid for strap, strap tabs, flap, and flap tab

⅜ yard of 58"-wide Soft and Stable (or Thermolam Plus fusible fleece)

1¼ yards of 20"-wide Shape-Flex fusible woven interfacing (or other medium-weight fusible interfacing)

2 metal swivel clips (¾" *or* 1")

2 metal D-rings (¾" *or* 1")

1 magnetic snap (½")

1 zipper, 14" long

Optional: 4 metal purse feet

Optional: metal rivets and tool for attaching them

CUTTING

The patterns for the main panel/lining pocket, side panel, flap, and flap tab are on pattern sheet 2.

From the purple print, cut:
2 main panels, *on fold,* for bag front and back
1 rectangle, 4" x 14", for bag bottom
2 side panels, *on fold*

From the gray print, cut:
2 main panels, *on fold,* for lining front and back
2 lining pockets, *on fold;* shorten the main-panel pattern as indicated before cutting
1 rectangle, 4" x 14", for lining bottom
2 side panels, *on fold,* for lining sides
1 rectangle, 2" x 4", for zipper tab

From the gray solid, cut:
1 rectangle, 3" x 36", for strap
2 flaps, *on fold*
2 flap tabs
4 rectangles, 1¼" x 3½", for strap tabs

From the Soft and Stable, cut:
2 main panels, *on fold,* for bag front and back*
1 rectangle, 4" x 14", for bag bottom
2 side panels, *on fold,* for bag sides*
1 flap, *on fold**

*Because the Soft and Stable is thick, you'll be able to cut more accurately if you prepare a full pattern from a folded piece of paper and use it to cut the stabilizer in a single layer without folding. You can also use the cut fabric, unfolded, as your pattern.

Continued on page 72

Metal rivets add a hint of shine to the front of the bag and also help secure the ends of the flap tab.

FIG. 1

↕ 1"

Continued from page 70

From the Shape-Flex, cut:
1 rectangle, 3" x 36", for strap
2 main panels, *on fold*, for lining front and back
1 rectangle, 4" x 14", for lining bottom
2 side panels, *on fold*, for lining sides
1 flap, *on fold*
2 flap tabs
4 rectangles, 1¼" x 3½", for strap tabs

ATTACH THE INTERFACING

1. **Place the wrong side of the bag front** against the corresponding piece of Soft and Stable and pin. Baste ⅛" from the edges. Repeat to baste Soft and Stable to one flap and the bag back, sides, and bottom.

2. **Following the manufacturer's instructions,** fuse the Shape-Flex pieces to the wrong side of the strap; lining front, back, bottom, and sides; flap tabs; strap tabs; and the second flap.

ASSEMBLE THE FLAP AND FLAP TAB

All seam allowances are ½" unless otherwise noted.

1. **Mark the snap placement** on the flap with Soft and Stable, 1" above the curved edge and centered from side to side. Install the ball half of the magnetic snap as instructed in "Magnetic Snaps" on page 88 **(fig. 1).**

2. **Pin the prepared flaps,** right sides together, and sew along the entire outer edge, using a ¼" seam allowance. Leave a 4" opening along one long edge.

3. **Trim the corners diagonally** and notch the seam allowances along the curves, being careful not to clip through the stitching. Turn the flap right side out and press it flat, pressing the seam allowances to the wrong side along the opening. Topstitch ⅛" from the outer edges, closing the opening as you stitch.

4. **Mark the placement for the magnetic snap** on the bag front, centered 5" below the top edge. Install the socket half of the snap at the mark.

5. **Pin the flap tabs right sides together,** and sew along the entire outer edge using a ¼" seam allowance. Leave a 3" opening along one long edge.

6. **Notch the seam allowances along the curves.** Turn the flap tab right side out and press it flat, pressing the seam allowances to the wrong side along the opening. Topstitch ⅛" from the outer edges, closing the opening as you stitch.

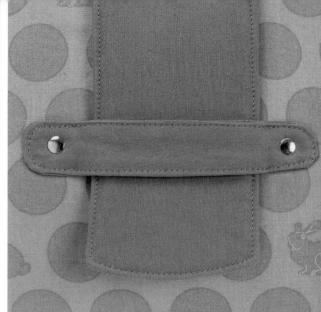

7. **With a removable marking tool,** draw a horizontal line on the bag front 3" below the top edge. Center the flap tab below that line, with its curved ends 3¾" from each side edge, giving the flap tab a slight lift in the center. Pin the ends of the flap tab to the bag front.

8. **Sew each end of the flap tab to the bag front,** beginning and ending the stitches 1" from the end of the tab, leaving the center open for the flap. Sew directly on top of the previous topstitches, and backstitch at each end of the seams to secure. *Optional:* Install a rivet ½" from each end of the flap tab, following the manufacturer's instructions **(fig. 2).**

9. **With a removable marking tool,** draw a horizontal line on the bag back 2¼" below the top edge. Center the flap above the line with the snap side face down. Topstitch ⅛" and ¼" from the short edge of the flap to secure it to the bag back **(fig. 3).**

10. **Fold the flap downward** against the bag back and pin it out of the way before continuing the bag's construction.

ATTACH THE ZIPPER

1. **Press ¼" to the wrong side** on both 4" edges of the zipper tab. Fold the zipper tab in half widthwise, wrong sides together, aligning the short ends, and press. Open the fold and press both raw edges to the wrong side so that they meet at the center crease. Refold along the original line and press once more so that all of the raw edges are enclosed.

2. **Slide the bottom end of the zipper into the zipper tab,** resting the ends of the zipper tape against the center crease, and pin. Topstitch ⅛" from all four edges of the zipper tab, securing the zipper. Stitch slowly and carefully over the zipper teeth to avoid breaking the needle.

FIG. 2

FIG. 3

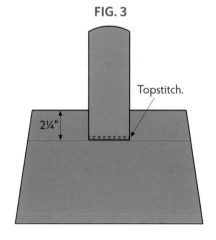

Topstitch.

FIG. 4

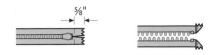

FIG. 5

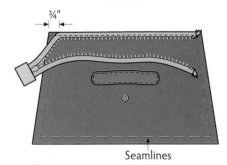

Seamlines

FIG. 6

FIG. 7

3. **Mark the wrong side of both zipper tapes** ⅝" from the upper end. Unzip the zipper. With the zipper wrong side up, fold each zipper tape end diagonally by bringing the center edge to meet the line you drew, and sew a few tacking stitches to keep the fold in place **(fig. 4)**.

4. **Place the zipper along the top edge of the bag front,** right sides together, with the open end of the zipper to the right. The diagonal fold should end at the raw edge of the bag front, positioning the top zipper stop just inside the side seamline. Pin the zipper to the bag front. Beginning ¾" from the left side of the bag front, bend the zipper tape downward slightly so the edge of the zipper tape falls outside the intersecting seam allowances at the corner. It may be helpful to pin the bottom of the zipper to the bag front so that it remains clear of the seam allowances in the next steps. Sew the zipper to the top edge of the bag front using a ¼" seam allowance **(fig. 5)**.

5. **Repeat step 5** to attach the other side of the zipper to the bag back, reversing references to left and right.

MAKE THE STRAP

1. **Press the strap in half lengthwise,** wrong sides together. Open the fold and press the long edges to the wrong side so that they meet at the center crease. Refold along the original crease and press once more. Topstitch ⅛" from each long edge.

2. **Press ½" to the wrong side** on each end of the strap. Press an additional 1" to the wrong side on each end. Slide a swivel clip onto each end of the strap, resting them in the second creases. Sew a small rectangle near the first fold on each end of the strap, enclosing the raw edges and securing the swivel clips.

3. **Sew two strap tabs,** wrong sides together, along both long edges, using a ¼" seam allowance. Turn the tab right side out and press it flat. Press ¾" to the wrong side on one short end. Fold the second end to the wrong side so that the raw edges meet and press again. Make two.

4. **Slide the straight edge of a D-ring** onto each strap tab, resting the ring in the ¾" fold **(fig. 6)**.

5. **With a tool that creates removable marks,** draw a line on each side panel 6½" above the bottom edge. Center the D-ring end of a prepared strap tab just below the line on each side panel, with the raw edges against the side panel, and pin.

6. **Using a zipper foot,** topstitch ⅛" from the side and lower edges of one strap tab. Pivot ¼" below the D-ring and sew across the tab to finish, overlapping the beginning and ending stitches for security. Repeat to stitch the second strap tab to the other side panel **(fig. 7)**.

ASSEMBLE THE BAG

1. *Optional:* **If you are using purse feet,** install them now, following the instructions in "Purse Feet" on page 89.

2. **Sew the bag bottom** to the lower edge of the bag front. Press the seam allowances toward the bag bottom. Sew the bag back to the other long edge of the bag bottom and press as before.

3. **Find and mark the bottom centers** of the bag unit and side panels. Matching the centers and aligning the raw edges at the top, pin a side panel to one side edge of the bag. Sew the side panel to the bag, easing the fabric around the curves. Notch the seam allowances to reduce bulk along the curves. Press the seam allowances toward the side panel. Repeat to attach the second side panel to the other side of the bag. **✱See "Sew Sensible," right.**

4. **Sew the lining pockets,** right sides together, along the top edge, using a ¼" seam allowance. Press the seam allowances open. Reposition the fabrics wrong sides together, folding along the seam and matching the raw edges, and press. Topstitch ⅛" from the seam.

5. **Pin the lining pocket** to the right side of the lining front, matching the side and bottom edges. Baste ¼" from the raw edges.

6. **Finger-press the unit in half** to find the vertical centerline. Topstitch on the crease from the top edge of the pocket to the bottom raw edge, dividing the pocket into two sections.

7. **Repeat steps 2 and 3** to assemble the lining. Leave a 6" opening in one bottom seam for turning.

FINISH THE BAG

1. **Turn the bag right side out.** Slide the lining over the bag so that they are right sides together, with the side seams and top edges aligned. Be sure that the zipper tail and flap are tucked inside, away from the raw edges, and pin. Stitch the top edge of the bag using a ¼" seam allowance.

2. **Turn the bag right side out** through the opening in the lining. Tuck the lining into the bag and press the top edge flat. Topstitch ⅛" from the top edge.

3. **Close the opening in the lining** with hand or machine stitches.

4. **Unpin the flap,** slide it through the flap tab, and snap it into place. Clip the strap onto the D-rings on the bag sides.

✱ *sew sensible*

Sew the side panel to the bag bottom first, and then stitch up the side seams to distribute the fabric evenly.

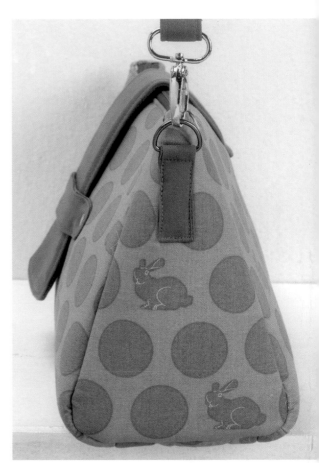

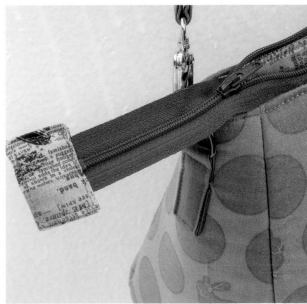

Shades Laptop Backpack

I designed this backpack with two men in mind, so it's created with unisex appeal. It's the perfect bag for a favorite high schooler or college student, with ample storage space in the front pocket for little gadgets and a main compartment sized to hold a small laptop.

FINISHED SIZE: 13½" x 16" x 5"

MATERIALS

Yardage is based on 54"-wide home-decor–weight fabric unless otherwise noted.

1 yard of cream print for exterior

1½ yards of 42"-wide black-and-blue print quilting cotton for lining

¼ yard of black solid for bag bottom

¾ yard of 58"-wide Soft and Stable (or Thermolam Plus fusible fleece)

3 yards of 20"-wide Shape-Flex fusible woven interfacing (or other medium-weight fusible interfacing)

1 yard of 24"-wide, ½"-thick foam

1 package (3 yards) of ½"-wide "extra-wide" double-fold bias tape (or make your own)*

1 zipper, 9" long

2 zippers, 36" long**

2 metal sliders (1½")

2 metal rectangular rings (1½")

If you prefer to make your own binding, purchase 1¾ yards of the lining fabric and cut bias strips 2" wide, totaling 108" when joined together, in addition to the pieces listed below.

**The sample bag uses outerwear zippers with molded plastic teeth and two zipper pulls. The double pulls mean the zipper can be opened from either end, a real plus. However, you can substitute any 36"-long regular or separating zipper in your bag.*

* fabric facts

The exterior is constructed from sturdy home-decor fabrics. If you prefer to use quilting cotton, purchase 1⅝ yards of exterior fabric and ⅜ yard of bag-bottom fabric, and add an extra layer of interfacing to the exterior and bag-bottom pieces for body. The ½"-thick foam is included to pad the bag and protect your laptop. If you won't be carrying a laptop, feel free to omit the foam.

CUTTING

The patterns for the main panel/laptop pocket and front pocket are on pattern sheet 4.

From the cream print, cut:

2 rectangles, 5" x 52", for straps

1 rectangle, 6" x 37½", for zipper panel

2 main panels, *on fold,* for bag front and back

1 front pocket; place the pattern right side up on the fabric right side*

2 squares, 5" x 5", for strap extenders

From the black-and-blue print, cut:

1 rectangle, 6" x 37½", for lining zipper panel

2 main panels, *on fold,* for lining front and back

2 laptop pockets, *on fold;* shorten the main-panel pattern as indicated before cutting

1 front pocket for front-pocket lining; place the pattern right side up on the fabric wrong side

1 rectangle, 10" x 20", for zippered pocket

2 rectangles, 6" x 10", for gadget divider

If your print is large, fussy cut the pocket so that the print flows continuously from the backpack onto the pocket, as in the sample bag.

Continued on page 78

* right side up

The front-pocket pattern is asymmetrical, so it's important to consider its direction when cutting the exterior, lining, and interfacing pieces. Be sure you follow the instructions under "Cutting." Soft and Stable has no right side, so it can be cut either way.

Continued from page 76

From the black solid, cut:
2 rectangles, 6" x 21", for bag and lining bottoms
1 rectangle, 3" x 10", for handle loop

From the Soft and Stable, cut:
2 main panels, *on fold,* for bag front and back**
1 rectangle, 6" x 37½", for zipper panel
1 rectangle, 6" x 21", for bag bottom
1 front pocket

From the Shape-Flex, cut:
2 rectangles, 5" x 52", for straps
2 main panels, *on fold,* for lining front and back
1 rectangle, 6" x 37½", for lining zipper panel
1 rectangle, 6" x 21", for lining bottom
1 front pocket; place the pattern right side up on the non-fusible
    side of the interfacing
2 squares, 5" x 5", for strap extenders
1 rectangle, 3" x 10", for handle loop

From the ½"-thick foam, cut:
2 main panels; before cutting, trace the main-panel pattern onto
    folded paper and cut away 1" from all sides (except the fold).
    Use the new pattern to cut 2 pieces of foam.
1 rectangle, 3¾" x 18"

**Because the Soft and Stable is thick, you'll be able to cut more*
accurately if you prepare a full pattern from a folded piece of paper and
use it to cut the stabilizer in a single layer without folding. You can also
use the cut fabric, unfolded, as your pattern.

ATTACH THE INTERFACING

1. **Place the wrong side of the bag front** against the corresponding piece of Soft and Stable and pin. Baste ⅛" from the edges. Repeat to baste Soft and Stable to the bag back, bag bottom, zipper panel, and front pocket.

2. **Following the manufacturer's instructions,** fuse the Shape-Flex pieces to the wrong side of the straps; lining zipper panel, bottom, front, and back; front pocket; handle loop; and strap extenders.

ASSEMBLE THE STRAP

All seam allowances are ½" unless otherwise noted.

1. **Fold one strap in half lengthwise** with wrong sides together and press. Open the fold and press both long edges to the wrong side so that they meet at the center crease. Refold along the original crease and press once more. Topstitch ⅛" from each long edge. Make two.

2. **Repeat step one** to make the handle loop and two strap extenders.

3. **Transfer the strap and strap-extender placement marks** to the bag back with a removable marking tool.

4. **Slide one rectangular ring** onto a strap extender. Fold the strap extender in half, matching the raw edges, and pin or baste. Position the strap extender on the bag back, right sides up, just inside one strap-extender placement mark, aligning the raw edges. Baste ¼" from the raw edges. Sew through all the layers ¼" below the rectangular ring to hold the strap extender in place against the bag back. Repeat to attach the remaining strap extender at the other placement mark.

5. **Baste one end of a strap** to the top edge of the bag back just inside one of the strap placement marks, angling the strap slightly toward the center of the bag. The strap and bag back should be right side up; baste ¼" from the bag raw edges **(fig. 1)**.

6. **Slide the strap's free end** through a slider, weaving it over the slider's center bar. Pass the strap end through the corresponding rectangular ring from front to back and then bring it back to the slider. Weave the strap end over the slider's center bar, underneath the other strap layer. Press ½" of the strap end to the wrong side and stitch the fold to the strap, 2½" from the slider, with a small rectangle of stitches that secures the free end of the strap and encloses the raw edges. See "Metal Slider for an Adjustable Strap" on page 91 for more information.

7. **Repeat steps 5 and 6** to attach the remaining strap.

8. **Fold the bag back in half** to find the center of its top edge. Mark the bag back ⅜" to each side of the center. Fold the handle loop in half, aligning the short ends side by side. Center the handle on the top edge of the bag back, spreading the handle ends apart so that they lie on the two marks and aligning the bag and handle raw edges. The fold in the handle will extend toward the center of the bag back and there will be a ¾" space between the two short ends. Baste ¼" from the raw edges **(fig. 2)**.

FIG. 1

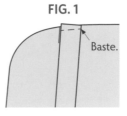

Baste.

FIG. 2

⅜"   ⅜"

Baste.

Center

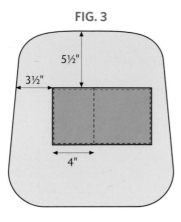

FIG. 3

5½"

3½"

4"

* pocket planner

Change the measurement of the pocket-dividing line to suit your preference for holding headphones or other gear.

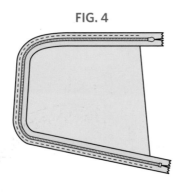

FIG. 4

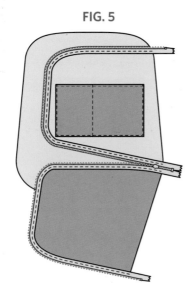

FIG. 5

MAKE THE FRONT POCKET

1. **Pin the two gadget dividers** right sides together, raw edges matched. Sew around the entire outer edge using a ¼" seam allowance, leaving a 6" opening near the center of the top 10" edge. Clip the corners diagonally and turn the divider right side out. Use a point turner or other tool to gently shape the corners and then press the divider flat, pressing the seam allowances to the wrong side along the opening. Topstitch ⅛" from the edges, closing the opening as you stitch.

2. **Mark the bag front 5½" below** the top edge and 3½" from the left edge. Pin the gadget divider to the bag front, matching the upper left corner to the mark. Be sure the divider is horizontally level by measuring 5½" from the top edge along the width of the divider. Sew the sides and bottom ⅛" from the divider edge, sewing directly on top of the previous stitches. Leave the top edge open.

3. **Measure and mark a vertical line** on the gadget divider, 4" from its left-hand edge. Stitch along the line, backstitching at the top and bottom to reinforce the seam (fig. 3). ***See "Pocket Planner," left.**

4. **Place the front-pocket pattern** on the bag front, 1½" below the top of the bag, with the right-hand edges matched. Trace along the pattern edge with a removable marking tool to mark the zipper placement.

5. **Pin one 36"-long zipper to the front pocket,** right sides together, along the top, bottom, and left edges. The zipper will be slightly longer than the pocket edge; use the extra length to plan ahead so that the zipper stops don't fall at the right-side seamline. Using a zipper foot, stitch the zipper to the pocket, sewing ¼" from the zipper teeth (fig. 4).

6. **Pin the pocket lining to the pocket,** right sides together, with the zipper sandwiched between. Sew directly on top of the previous stitches. Notch the pocket and lining seam allowances along the curves to reduce bulk, being careful not to cut into the zipper tape or the stitches. Turn the pocket right side out through the open edge and press the zipper away from the pocket. Topstitch the pocket ⅛" from the seamline. Baste ⅛" from the raw edges.

7. **Unzip the zipper.** Pin the free side of the zipper to the bag front, right sides together, positioning the zipper teeth just inside the guideline. Stitch ¼" from the zipper teeth. Close the zipper, keeping the zipper pull within the pocket area, and take a few tacking stitches across the zipper teeth ¼" from the bag's raw edge. Trim the zipper to match the bag edges (fig. 5).

8. **Baste the raw edge of the pocket** to the bag front, ⅛" from the raw edges.

ASSEMBLE THE ZIPPER PANEL

1. **Draw a line on the wrong side of the zipper panel,** 2¾" from one long edge. Draw a second line ½" below the first. Draw additional lines 2¼" from each short end, forming a narrow rectangle at the center of the zipper panel **(fig. 6).**

2. **Place the zipper panel** and lining zipper panel right sides together, matching the raw edges, and pin. Sew along the rectangular box, directly on top of the lines.

3. **Continue assembling the zipper panel** as if it were a zippered pocket, omitting references to the pocket piece, and using the second 36"-long zipper. See "Zippered Pocket" on page 86. You will end with a zipper set into a window at the center of the lined zipper panel.

4. **Align the raw edges of the zipper panel** and its lining. Baste ⅛" from the long edges, leaving 4" at each end free.

5. **Fold the assembled zipper panel in half,** matching the short edges. Measure and mark the *folded* edge 1" from each side. Mark each side edge 9" below the fold. Connect the marks on each side with a diagonal line. Cut along the lines. Baste the fabric to the stabilizer ⅛" from each of the newly cut edges (fig. 7).

6. **Pull the lining zipper panel away** from the exterior zipper panel at one short end. Match the exterior zipper panel to one end of the bag bottom, right sides together, and pin. Sew along the pinned edge, keeping the lining panel free. Press the seam allowances open. Repeat to attach the other end of the bag bottom to the other end of the bag zipper panel, and then sew the lining bottom to the lining zipper panel in the same way, creating a loop of fabric with the panels wrong sides together. (fig. 8).

7. **Stitch in the ditch** of the zipper panel/bottom seams to hold the layers together, creating a pocket for the foam padding. Slide the rectangular piece of foam between the bag and lining bottoms. Baste ⅛" from the raw edges to hold the foam in place.

FIG. 6

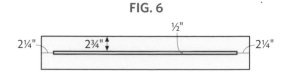

2¼"   2¾"   ½"   2¼"

FIG. 7

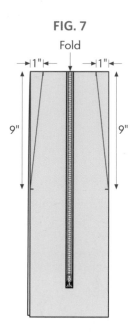

Fold

1"   1"

9"   9"

FIG. 8

FIG. 9

Center

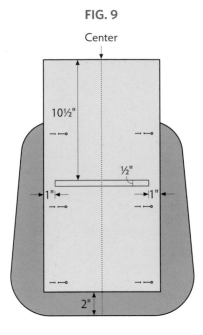

10½"

½"

1"   1"

2"

* through thick and thin

The last few steps require patience as you sew through many fabric layers. Sew slowly. Change to a denim or jeans needle with a sharp point in size 90/14 or 100/16 for easier going.

If your binding isn't perfect, don't be distressed. When the bag is turned right side out, the binding will be recessed into the corners of the bag and largely invisible.

FIG. 10

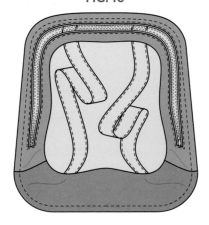

ASSEMBLE THE ZIPPERED POCKET

1. **On the wrong side of the zippered pocket,** measure and mark a horizontal line 10½" below the top 10" edge. Draw a second line ½" below the first.

2. **Draw a vertical line 1"** from each side edge, connecting the horizontal lines to form a narrow rectangular box.

3. **Finger-press the lining front and pocket** to find their vertical centerlines. Pin the pocket to the lining front, right sides together and centerlines matched, with the bottom edge of the pocket 2" above the bottom of the lining front **(fig. 9)**.

4. **Follow the instructions in "Zippered Pocket"** on page 86 to install the 9"-long zipper and complete the pocket.

MAKE THE LAPTOP POCKET

1. **Pin the two laptop pocket pieces** right sides together and sew ¼" from the straight edge. Turn the pocket right side out, folding it along the seamline, and press it flat. Topstitch ¼" from the finished edge.

2. **Place the laptop pocket** on the lining back, right sides up, matching the sides and lower edges. Baste ¼" from the raw edges.

FINISH THE BAG

1. **Place the lining back on the bag back,** wrong sides together, sandwiching one piece of ½"-thick foam between the fabric layers. Baste ⅛" from the raw edges. Repeat with the bag and lining fronts and the second piece of foam.

2. **Unzip the zipper in the zipper panel.** Find and mark the top and bottom centers on the bag front and back and the zipper/bottom panel. Pin one long edge of the zipper/bottom panel to the bag back, exterior sides together. Align the top and bottom centers, and place the seams between the zipper panel and bottom at the notches on the bag back. Be sure the straps are folded into the center of the bag, away from the seam. Sew the bag back to the zipper/bottom panel, easing as necessary. Sew the bag front to the free edge of the zipper/bottom panel in the same way **(fig. 10)**. ✳ **See "Through Thick and Thin," left.**

3. **Cut two pieces of double-fold bias tape,** each 54" long. Open one end of each piece and press the end to the wrong side at a 45° angle. Refold the binding along the original creases.

4. **Beginning with the angled end,** slip one piece of binding over an unfinished bag seam allowance. Pin the binding over the entire length of the seam, back to the angled end of the binding. Trim the excess binding, leaving a 1" overlap, and slide the unfinished end of the binding inside the pressed end to enclose the raw edge. Topstitch the binding to the seam allowances, catching both binding edges and enclosing all the raw edges of the fabric. Repeat to bind the second seam with the remaining piece of binding. ✳**See "Keep It Taut," right.**

5. **Turn the bag right side out** and press well. Fold the bag, wrong sides together, along one seam at a time and press with steam. You may also use a wooden clapper to flatten the seams.

✳ keep it taut

As you pin the binding to the seam allowances, pull the binding gently so that it is taut to prevent ripples and puckers. If you are a quilter, you may prefer to sew and flip the binding as if on a quilt, finishing its second edge by hand. One of my pattern testers recommends using ¼"-wide fusible-web tape to hold the binding in place for sewing.

INTERFACING CONVERSIONS

PELLON	VILENE
Fusible Thermolam Plus (TP971F; green label)	Iron-On High-Loft Fleece (H640) or Thermolam Plus (272)
Shape-Flex (SF 101; pink label)	Woven Fusible (G700)
Peltex Sew-In Ultra Firm Stabilizer (70; yellow label)	Heavy Sew-In (S80)
Décor Bond (809)	Iron-On (H250)

* finely fused

I like to press Thermolam Plus with the fabric right side up on top of the fleece, using a mist of water on the fabric. When I'm sure it's properly fused, I flip the layers over and press again on top of the fleece. This leaves the fabric incredibly flat and smooth.

One of my favorite topics is interfacing; you really cannot make a bag without it. Interfacing makes up 25% of my fabric stash . . . no lie! It's one of those things that you just need to have on hand at all times, because you'll use it in almost every project.

I often use Pellon interfacing. If you live in a country where Pellon is not available, you may have luck finding the European brand Vilene, which is a fine alternative for making bags. Refer to the interfacing conversion chart at left (which I put together with help from the lovely folks at Pellon).

Most of my favorite interfacings are fusible. When fusing interfacing to your fabric, always use a pressing cloth to protect the fabric from excessive heat and keep the adhesive off your iron. Always place the bumpy or tacky side of the interfacing against the wrong side of the fabric. *See "Needed Know-How," page 85.

FUSIBLE THERMOLAM PLUS (PELLON TP971F)

I absolutely love Thermolam Plus, a needled fleece that is denser and flatter than generic fusible fleece. When I'm making a bag or other accessory, I like it to have body; even for a simple tote bag, just two layers of fabric is too thin for me. This is a matter of personal preference, but I want my bags to have some substance and be able to carry 20 pounds without tearing at the bottom. I use Thermolam Plus fused to the bag's exterior fabric, sometimes in combination with either Shape-Flex or fusible fleece fused to the bag's lining fabric.

Thermolam Plus, once fused, leaves the fabric looking nice and smooth. Test a small piece on your exterior fabric; depending on your iron, you may need to apply heat longer than the manufacturer recommends, but be careful not to damage the fabric. Sometimes I leave the iron in place up to double the recommended time. *See "Finely Fused," left.

SHAPE-FLEX (PELLON SF101)

I use Shape-Flex, a fusible woven interfacing, in all of my bags. It is the most important interfacing in my stash, and I rely on it for a variety of uses. I fuse woven interfacing to every pocket I make, and I use it to reinforce the area around a zipper.

Once fused, Shape-Flex gives quilting-weight cotton the sturdy feel of a home-decor or canvas-weight fabric. Place the rough, tacky side against the fabric's wrong side for fusing. Shape-Flex is perfect as a stand-alone interfacing in a pouch or other small project, or you can combine it with other interfacings.

PELTEX SEW-IN (PELLON 70)

This stiff interfacing is good for adding firm body without too much thickness. Because it is a sew-in interfacing, it will not fuse to your fabric. You can baste the interfacing to the fabric ⅛" inside the seam allowance, but I prefer this alternate method:

Cut one piece each of Shape-Flex and Peltex Sew-In the same size as the pattern piece. Trim ½" from the edges of the Peltex Sew-In. Center the Peltex Sew-In on the wrong side of the fabric and then place the Shape-Flex on top with its fusible side down. When you fuse the Shape-Flex, it will seal the Peltex Sew-In to the fabric along the ½" edges. Using a smaller piece of Peltex Sew-In also reduces the bulk of the seam allowance.

DÉCOR BOND (PELLON 809)

When there are bag panels or handles that need to look stiff without crinkling at folds and creases, this is the interfacing to use.

My favorite application is to use this interfacing in two layers. First, I fuse a layer of Shape-Flex against the wrong side of my fabric, and then I add two layers of Décor Bond, cutting the Décor Bond ½" smaller on all its edges to keep bulk out of the seam allowances. One or two layers of Décor Bond will help a bag stand up by itself, but without quite as much stiffness as you'll get with Peltex Sew-In.

BYANNIE'S SOFT AND STABLE

A ⅛"-thick foam interfacing, Soft and Stable has thin coatings on both sides so it feeds easily through your sewing machine. Amazingly, it makes any bag stand up by itself, but because it's not rigid, it's also easy to fit through a sewing machine while you are stitching. It's my favorite interfacing. As an alternative, try either Bosal In-R-Foam or Pellon Flex Foam (see "Resources" on page 95).

To apply this interfacing to the wrong side of the bag fabric, baste it by stitching ⅛" from the edges. Don't use a basting spray, which can contribute to a crinkled appearance in the finished bag. I like to gently pull my fabric taut as I am basting it to the Soft and Stable for a tight, crisp finish. If you like, you can machine quilt the Soft and Stable to your fabric after basting.

There are no hard-and-fast rules for using interfacing. I suggest that the best way to learn more about interfacing is to use it in all of your projects. Tweak your interfacing choice based on your personal preference: what kind of shape are you interested in, how much stiffness, what kind of body? There are unlimited possibilities!

*it's a wonder

If you don't have interfacing handy, Pellon Wonder Under (a fusible web) will turn any fabric into a fusible interfacing. For example, you can use fusible web to adhere a piece of canvas or batting to your quilting cotton, adding lots of body.

*needed know-how

Whenever you're fusing interfacing to fabric, follow the manufacturer's instructions carefully for product-specific guidelines. This is my favorite general-purpose method, especially when I'm using Shape-Flex:

Place the fabric, right side down, on the pressing surface. Add the interfacing, fusible side down, and cover both with a pressing cloth. Lightly spritz the pressing cloth with water.

Press with the iron, using an up-and-down motion rather than sliding. Overlap the pressing areas, holding the iron in place for approximately 10 seconds at each spot. When you're finished, allow the interfacing to cool completely. It should be firmly attached to your fabric.

Bag-Making Techniques

Details make all the difference in creating a bag that you'll be proud to flaunt. Use these helpful techniques to add professional polish to every bag you make!

* top tip

I like to draw a little T on the fabric's wrong side at the top of zippered pockets to avoid confusion later on.

This section explains how to use the purse hardware, piping, and other notions described in this book. You'll be able to apply these techniques to almost any bag that you wish to make, so this chapter is fantastic groundwork for your future as a bag maker!

ZIPPERED POCKET

This method for inserting a zipper to close a pocket is my favorite. I sometimes use the same technique for adding a zippered closure to the top of a bag, such as the Jump-Start Duffel or the Shades Laptop Backpack. While there are other ways to add a zipper, this is the fastest and easiest.

1. Cut the pocket fabric as directed in the project instructions. The patterns in this book commonly use 10" x 20" pocket fabric, so those dimensions are used in this example; alter the cut size as needed. **＊See "Top Tip," below left.**

2. Place the pocket piece, wrong side up, with one 10" edge at the top. Draw a horizontal line on the wrong side, 10½" below the top edge. Draw a second horizontal line ½" below the first **(fig. 1)**.

3. Draw short vertical lines between the horizontal lines and 1" from each side edge **(fig. 2)**.

FIG. 1

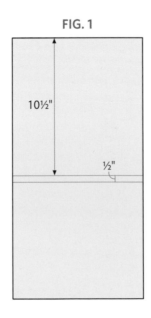

10½"

½"

FIG. 2

1"　　1"

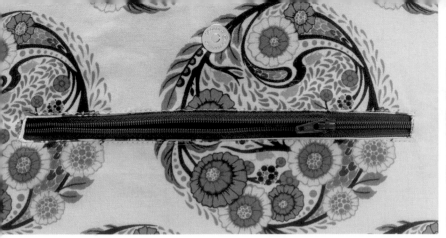

4. Finger-press the pocket and bag piece in half to find their centers. Place the pocket on the bag, right sides together, aligning the center creases. The bottom of the pocket should be at least ½" above the bottom edge of the bag; this will vary depending on the desired zipper location in your bag. Pin the layers together to avoid shifting.

5. Sew directly on the lines, creating a long, thin rectangular box (fig. 3).

6. Draw a line along the horizontal center of the rectangle, starting and stopping ¼" from the ends of the box. Draw diagonal lines into each corner, creating a small V at each end. Cut along the lines through both fabric layers, making sure not to cut into the stitching. A seam ripper is useful for starting the cut (fig. 4). ✳ See "V Careful," right.

7. Turn the pocket to the wrong side of the bag fabric through the opening and press (fig. 5). ✳ See "Is Thin In?," right.

✳ *v careful*

The farther you snip into the corners without cutting into the stitching, the sharper your pocket opening's corners will be, making for a professional look.

✳ *is thin in?*

For a less-bulky appearance around the zipper, you may choose to cut away the interfacing inside the rectangular "window" (plan ahead if necessary, and trim the interfacing before fusing). I prefer to leave the interfacing in place, using the slight bulk to highlight the zipper.

FIG. 3
Center

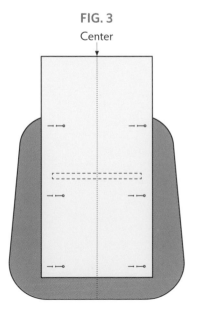

FIG. 4

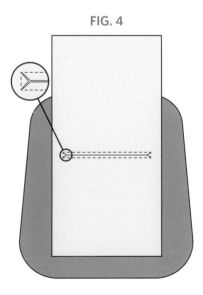

FIG. 5

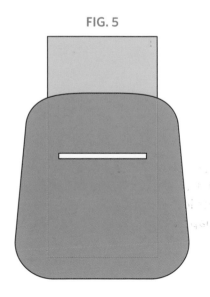

* zippy basting

Use basting tape or Elmer's glue instead of pins to temporarily adhere the zipper to the bag before edgestitching. If you use glue, set it with a hot, dry iron before stitching.

FIG. 6

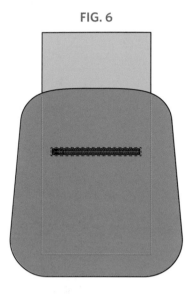

FIG. 7

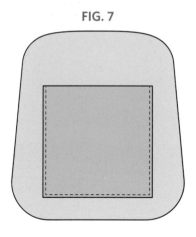

* sealed for security

I like to put a dab of seam sealant on the slits cut in the bag and lining fabrics before proceeding with the snap installation.

8. With the bag fabric right side up, center the zipper (also right side up) underneath the opening and pin it in place. Make sure that the pocket is lying flat and away from the opening. **✳ See "Zippy Basting," left.**

9. Using a zipper foot, edgestitch around the opening, ⅛" from the fabric edge, sewing the zipper in place (fig. 6).

10. Fold the pocket in half, right sides together, matching the edges and corners. Sew ¼" from the side and bottom edges of the pocket, keeping the bag fabric out of the seam (fig. 7).

MAGNETIC SNAPS

I use magnetic snaps often for flap closures, like the one on Woodson, and sometimes as a top closure in the lining of a bag, such as in Delilah. They are very simple to install.

1. Prepare the bag fabric with interfacing. Also cut two small squares of batting or fusible fleece to reinforce the bag fabric for regular use.

2. With a removable marking tool or chalk, mark prong placements as directed in your pattern. Also mark prong placements at the centers of the reinforcement squares. If the snap set includes washers, use one as a stencil for the placement markings; if not, use the thinner half of the snap (with the raised center) as a guide. Cut a small slit at each mark. **✳ See "Sealed for Security," below left.**

3. Slide the prongs of the snap through the slits from the right side of the fabric. Place the fleece or batting, then the washer (if included with the snap), over the prongs. Fold the prongs outward, making sure they lie flat against the bag fabric and reinforcement (fig. 8).

4. Repeat the process to insert the other half of the magnetic snap in the specified bag or lining piece.

FIG. 8

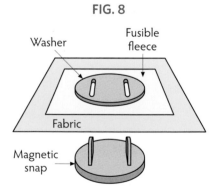

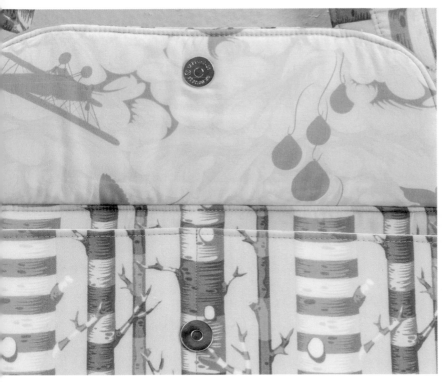

PURSE FEET

Purse feet are inexpensive and easy to install. They can be added to any bag with a flat bottom, but should be installed before you assemble the bag.

1. With a removable marking tool, draw lines on the wrong side of the prepared bag bottom, 1½" from each edge or as directed. Cut four 2" squares of fleece or batting to reinforce the bag fabric, one for each foot location.

2. Make a small slit at each of the four corners where the lines intersect. I recommend reinforcing the slits in the fabric with a small dab of seam sealant.

3. Slide one metal purse foot through a slit from the right side of the fabric.

4. To reinforce the fabric, cut a slit in the center of a piece of fleece or batting and slide it onto the prongs, against the wrong side of the fabric. Open the prongs outward.

5. Repeat the process to insert the remaining feet (fig. 9).

FIG. 9

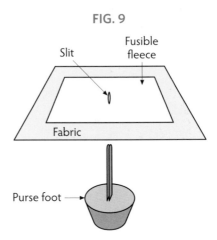

For more tips on using purse hardware, including how-to videos, check out my website: www.sewsweetness.com /purseware

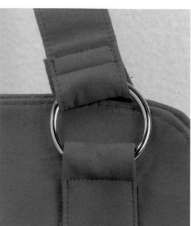

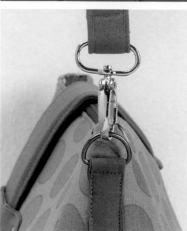

FIG. 10

METAL RINGS AND SWIVEL CLIPS

Metal hardware is usually available in several sizes and finishes. It's used for attaching straps to a bag, and the method for installing any of the pieces is the same.

1. Assemble the handle or strap as directed in the project instructions.

2. Press ½" to the wrong side on each end of the handle. Press an additional 1" to the wrong side on each end, or as otherwise directed for your project.

3. Slide one end of the handle through the hardware so that the ring lies in the second crease. Sew a small rectangle near the first fold, enclosing the raw edges and securing the hardware (fig. 10).

METAL SLIDER FOR AN ADJUSTABLE STRAP

I love an adjustable strap, because it can take any bag from handbag to cross-body bag. This technique requires a sewn strap piece, another piece (the strap extender) that is the same width as the strap and at least 4" long, and the slider plus a rectangular ring (fig. 11).

1. Construct the strap and strap extender as instructed for the specific project, enclosing all the long raw edges.

2. Slide the rectangular ring to the middle of the strap extender. Fold the extender in half around the ring, matching the raw edges, and position it on one side of the bag's upper edge. Baste the layers together ¼" from the raw edges.

3. Baste one end of the strap to the side of the bag opposite the strap extender. Weave the free end of the strap through the slider, passing over the slider's center bar. Pass the strap end through the rectangular ring from right side to wrong side (fig. 12).

4. Press ½" to the wrong side on the free end of the strap, and then press an additional 1½" to the wrong side. Wrap the strap end around the slider's center bar, underneath the previously woven strap, so that the bar rests in the second pressed fold. Be sure the strap is not twisted. Sew a small rectangle through the strap end near the first fold, enclosing the raw edges and securing the hardware (fig. 13).

PIPING

Piping really takes a bag to the next level. I use it either along the side panels or around the front and back of a bag. You can add piping to any bag, even if it isn't called for in the pattern. With a little bit of Wonder Under fusible-web tape, installing the piping will be a snap!

In this example, I'm using ⁵⁄₃₂"-diameter cording on a pattern with ½" seam allowances. If your cording or pattern differ, you may need to recalculate the width of the strips you cut.

1. Cut 1½"-wide strips on the bias as directed in the pattern; the combined length of the strips must equal the length of the seams where piping will be inserted, plus a few inches for seam allowance and ease. You'll also need ⁵⁄₃₂"-diameter cotton cording (the length of the piped seams plus about 10") and Pellon Wonder Under paper-backed fusible-web tape (or fusible web yardage cut into ½"-wide strips). *See "Cut It Right," right.

2. Prepare the interfaced pieces for your bag as directed in the pattern. In this example, I am applying the piping to the bag front and back.

FIG. 11

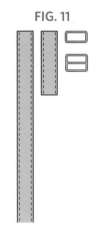

FIG. 12

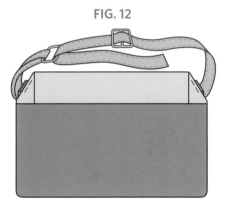

FIG. 13

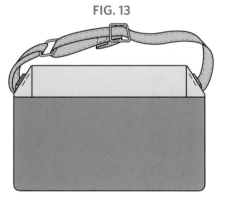

*cut it right

"On the bias" means that the strips are cut on a 45° angle to the selvage. Most quilting rulers have an angled line indicating the correct angle.

* the big chill

It's very important that the Wonder Under is completely cool before you attempt to remove the paper backing. If not, you'll find it very difficult to pull the paper cleanly away from the fabric.

FIG. 14

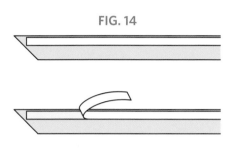

FIG. 15

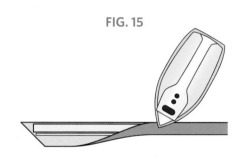

* top piping

For a bag with a separate side panel like "Trompe le Monde" on page 56, I prefer to keep the piping out of the seam allowances across the top of the bag. To accomplish this smoothly, pin or clip the piping to the fabric at an angle near the top edge, so that the last ½" to ¾" of piping on each side tapers off the fabric edge.

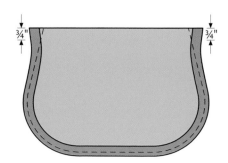

3. Join the bias strips into a continuous length with diagonal seams. Place two strips right sides together with the ends overlapping at a right angle. You'll notice that the overlapped area is a square. Sew across the square from corner to corner, trim the seam allowances to ¼", and press the seam allowances open. You may find that your bias strips already have angled ends; in that case, place the two strips at right angles with the diagonal ends matched and sew using a ¼" seam allowance. Continue in the same manner to join all the strips.

4. Fuse the Wonder Under tape to the wrong side of the joined strip along one long edge. Be sure the rough side of the fusible tape is against the fabric, and fuse it completely (several seconds on each segment). Remove the paper backing from the fusible tape (fig. 14). **✳ See "The Big Chill," above left.**

5. Lay the cotton cording in the center of the bias tape and fold the fabric around the cording, wrong sides together, matching the long edges. Start at one end and press slowly with the tip of the iron right against the cording to fuse the fabric snugly around the cord. Keep the cording in the center of the bias-cut fabric (fig. 15).

6. Pin or clip the prepared piping to the raw edges of the bag fabric, aligning the raw edges of the piping with the fabric edges. The cording should lie just inside the seamline. **✳ See "Top Piping," left.**

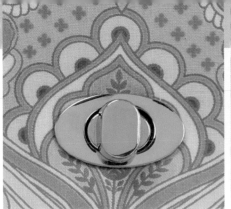

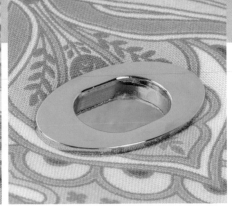

7. Baste the piping in place using a ¼" seam allowance. The fusible web holds the cording snugly inside the bias tape, so there is no need to sew any closer to the cord. ✳ See "Best Foot Forward," right.

8. Sew the bag pieces together with the basted piping in between. Use a ½" seam allowance and stitch the seam as usual. Because the seam allowance and cording math have already been calculated, following the seam line is all that's needed to create perfect piping.

TWIST LOCKS

A twist lock adds a bit of sparkle to a bag, and Festival on page 42 uses a twist lock in fantastic style. There are two different types of twist-lock installations: screw and prongs, and the two may be combined in one lock set. Always read and follow the manufacturer's specific instructions when installing your twist lock.

1. Assemble the bag flap and then mark a dot on the flap exterior, centered 1" above the lower edge (or as directed in the pattern). Center the oval frame of the twist lock over the dot and trace the screw placements and the central hole. Use an awl to make a hole in the fabric at each screw placement, and cut out the central hole. Place the oval back onto the fabric and use the screws to tighten the twist lock into place. If desired, apply a small amount of fabric glue inside the ridge of the oval frame and adhere it to the fabric, applying gentle pressure for several minutes. ✳ See "Prong Procedure," right.

2. Mark a dot on the bag front, centered under the location of the lock frame when the flap is closed. Center the twist lock over the dot and mark the prong or screw placements. Cut a small slit or hole at each placement mark and apply seam sealant to the openings. Repeat the process to draw and cut two openings in a 2" square of fleece or batting.

3. Insert the locking piece from the bag's right side. Slide the fleece or batting square onto the prongs or screws, followed by the washer (if one is included with the twist lock). Open the prongs outward to lie against the bag wrong side, or tighten the screws to hold the lock in place.

✳ *best foot forward*

Special piping feet are available for some machines, but because my bags use interfacing (such as thick Soft and Stable) it's difficult to feel the cording through the layers of fabric. I use a regular presser foot instead; you can also experiment with a zipper foot.

✳ *prong procedure*

If your twist lock has prongs at the back of its frame, mark the prong placements instead of screw holes and cut slits in the fabric to accommodate the prongs. Insert them through the flap and flatten the prongs against the back of the flap.

Choosing Fabric

Fabric plays a very important role in the bags that I make. Sometimes I select a bag pattern specifically to feature a fabric print I want to use, choosing a pattern that features the fabric well. Other times it's the opposite: I know which pattern I want to make, and I sort through my fabric stash to find the perfect fabric, one with a print scaled to work well with the bag's details.

COLORWAYS

There are so many great fabrics out there, I just can't stop making bags! To help inspire you, below are additional colorways of each of the bags in the book. Compare them with the originals to see how switching up the fabric really makes each bag unique!

PAGE 6

PAGE 12

PAGE 19

PAGE 25

PAGE 31

PAGE 36

PAGE 42

PAGE 48

PAGE 56

PAGE 64

PAGE 70

PAGE 76

Resources

Here's where I love to shop for fabric and bag-making supplies.

FABRIC

Crimson Tate:
www.crimsontate.com

Fat Quarter Shop:
www.fatquartershop.com

I Heart Tula Pink:
www.ihearttulapink.com

Pink Castle Fabrics:
www.pinkcastlefabrics.com

Stash Fabrics:
www.stashfabrics.com

INTERFACING

Bosal: www.bosalonline.com

ByAnnie's Soft and Stable:
www.byannie.com

Pellon: www.pellonprojects.com

PURSE HARDWARE

Sew Sweetness Purseware:
This is my own brand of hardware, which perfectly pairs with my bag patterns. www.sewsweetness.com /purseware

SEWING MACHINE

Juki: I sew on a Juki TL-2010Q sewing machine. It is a straight-stitch-only metal sewing machine. www.sewvacdirect.com

THREAD

Aurifil: www.aurifil.com

acknowledgments

To Danny, William, and Violet, thank you for loving me even though I am a bit neurotic about the sewing sometimes. I'm trying to learn to be more relaxed about it, I promise.

To my mom, dad, and grandparents, for being my biggest cheerleaders. When we go out to eat, my dad likes to tell servers that I have an Aurifil thread collection—as if they know what that means!

To my best friend, Kim, for always having my back and telling me what to do when I am overextended and just cannot think for one more second. She's the best business manager in the entire world!

To Kay Whitt, my mentor from the start. You are the epitome of the pattern designer, I will never have tears or a half-finished garment thrown into the trash when working from one of your amazing patterns.

To my incredible pattern testers, who each made a bag for this book in much-loved fabrics from my stash: Rebekah Bills, Holly Boyter, Pam Cobb, Wendy Dunham, Terry Druga, Cyndi Farfsing, Tiffany Fischer, Cheree Frank, Cindy Guch, Anna Lankeshofer, Holli Lofgren, and Jacqueline Maxman. I couldn't have done it without your beautiful sewing and quick eyes!

To Tula Pink, for sending me fabric for new patterns and for your encouragement. Thanks also to Cameron and Kat, for putting up with my emails and folding my fabric from I Heart Tula Pink like Gap employees.

To Erin, Cris, and all the folks at Pellon, who had my back from the very beginning. To Annie and Kaitlyn from ByAnnie, for your support ever since I stumbled upon Soft and Stable.

Thank you to Karen Burns, Mary Burns, Karen Soltys, Rebecca Kemp Brent, and everyone else at Martingale.

Julie Herman, Rachael Pannepacker, Alex Veronelli, Roseann Kermes, Pat Sloan, Bari J., Brenda Ratliff and Jason Elliott, Heather Givens and David Barnhouse, Quilt Jane, Emily Lang, Kate Whitsell: you are all amazing.

I could truly write a book of just thank-yous. I wish I could name you all, my faithful blog readers, for sending me comments and email that make my day. Thank you to everyone in the sewing industry who has given their time and expertise to help this girl figure out what to do, how to fix that problem, and to calm me down when I was worried.

Thank you, dear reader, for picking up this book. I'm going to hold you to the promise that you'll email me photos of your finished bags.

About the Author

SARA LAWSON lives in Chicago, Illinois, with her husband and two children. She started her blog on a whim in September 2010, and established her pattern company, Sew Sweetness, in 2013. Sara loves all things sewing and enjoys making bags, quilts, and garments. Her first book, *Big-City Bags,* was published by Martingale in November of 2013.